"HOW TO OUTSMART THE CREDIT BUREAUS"

Everything
You Ever Needed To
Know About
Credit Bureaus

Published by The Credo Company — Memphis, TN

Copyright © 2006 by The Credo Company, LLC
All rights reserved.

Editor: Chandra Sparks Taylor
www.chandrasparkstaylor.com

Cover design: Felix Walker

Book design: Essex Graphix
www.essexgraphix.com

Library of Congress Catalog Card Number: 00047-589
Library of Congress Control Number: 2006921026

ISBN:0-9767208-0-9

Printed in the United States of America.

The Credo Company
4466 Elvis Presley Blvd., Ste. 260
Memphis, TN 38116

thecredocompany@bellsouth.net
www.credocompany.com

AUTHOR STATEMENT

I am a person who believes in the power of faith in God and yourself.

Albert Einstein once said, "Imagination is greater than knowledge because it is infinite." I disagree. I think that a person can dream and imagine a different circumstance his entire life, but without knowledge he will never find a way out of his situation. There are many people who do not know where they stand in life simply because they have no knowledge about themselves. They do not understand how powerful they can become. How a person is born depends on the favor of God. How a person dies depends on how he uses the favor that God has given him. You may be born a pawn, but you can die a queen. For those who disagree with the information I have provided in this book, think about people who are born every day into poverty in the richest country in the world. Where there is poverty, there is crime. Where there is crime, there is ignorance. Where there is ignorance, there are those seeking to exploit that ignorance. This keeps many at the finish line of life, even before they can begin to start the race and accomplish their dreams.

TABLE OF CONTENTS

INTRODUCTION

Merriam Webster defines credit as the favorable estimate of a person's character, reputation, or good name. My definition is the accumulation of debt for the purpose of creating a good name. I do not think that Webster's calculated or considered the trials and financial problems that a person may face during the struggle of trying to live. I am sure there will be many upstanding individuals who will not agree with some of the practices and procedures I have disclosed throughout this book, but I guarantee that these people are having no problem obtaining credit for the purpose of feeling like they have a good name. What I mean by this is most of us feel a sense of pride when we apply for credit and receive it, as opposed to feeling embarrassed or disappointed when we do not.

Most people do not realize that credit bureaus are in the business of making money, just like any other company. All three are listed on the New York Stock Exchange. Have you ever considered that credit bureaus are monopolies? They have no morals, ethics, or respect for any laws put in place to govern their establishments. Do you think the regulators are enforcing any laws? If they were, then thirty-five percent of the population would not have bad credit.

Credit bureaus are nothing more than big corporations that are in bed with the government to contain the economically deprived and the financially illiterate individuals who work every day only to make the rich richer. It is bigger than slavery because all the disposable income that these individuals produce goes to the banks, insurance companies, and the credit bureaus.

I would like to offer you a quote from Julius Wilson: "The culture of poverty is both an adaptation and a reaction of the poor to their marginal position and class stratified, highly individuated capitalistic society. The culture of poverty tends to perpetuate itself from generation to generation because of its effect on the children. By the time poor children are age six or seven, they have usually absorbed the basic values and attitudes of their subculture and are not psychologically geared to take full advantage of changing conditions or increased opportunities which may occur in their lifetime." In other words, the rich get richer and the poor are trained by the rich to believe they are meant to remain poor. This means they are not seeking ways to outsmart the rich. Those individuals who are afraid to take the risk of advancing in life because of the fear that their risk is only a failure waiting to manifest itself will forever remain a slave to those who control politics, public school systems, corporations, and churches.

There are many things to be learned from the American economy. Some of these lessons are unforgiving. This book is meant to be a guide and a server of information as it relates to names and credit. The bureaus have been a monument of anxiety, frustration, happiness, fear, and most of all puzzlement for many since the beginning of their existence.

I have researched them for three years, devouring their computer systems and their laws. I have come to realize that computers are only as smart as the individuals who create them, and with that in mind, I am reminded of that old cliché, "There is always someone out there who is smarter than you." I wanted to be the individual who was smarter than the person who designed the computer systems for the credit bureaus. You see, any system can be broken, if you figure out which link holds the chain together.

When I began putting together a guide to help people overcome the stress of having bad credit, I was not doing it for the purpose of earning money or taking advantage of those individuals who are ignorant to what to do. Before I began explaining or exposing the secrets that credit bureaus do not want you to know, let me just say that you must have a positive attitude as well as an open mind in order to put my instructions to work. For people to be successful at anything, they must have a positive and optimistic attitude. If you have a negative mindset, then it will produce a negative result. Please when reading this book understand that everything that I have provided has been tried and proven.

THE HISTORY OF CREDIT BUREAUS

The only way to defeat any enemy is to know where he is as well as who he is and the weapons he has at his disposal. I'm going to give you a brief history of the three credit bureaus and the people who control them. There is no better way to gain social control over a population than information. This can be used as a defense or an offense. It can be used to create hope as well as fear.

Let us first examine Experian, which is not even an American company. Experian's history dates back to 1897 when James Chilton helped a Dallas company record its customers' credit information in notebooks. The Chilton Corporation was a credit reporting agency that was acquired by TRW Information Systems and Services in 1989. TRW dates back to 1958 when Thompson Machine Products purchased Ramo Woolridge, an aerospace company headquarted in Los Angeles. Ramo Woolridge changed its name to TRW and was involved in many defense contracts. It was a major part of the military industrial complex. In 1996, TRW sold its information systems and services to Tom Lee and Bain Capital Inc. for $1.1 billion. That same year Tom Lee renamed the company Experian and sold it to Great Universal Stores (GUS) for $1.7 billion. Great Universal Stores is a one-hundred-year-old British holding company located in the United Kingdom. It also owns CCN Group, Europe's largest credit reporting agency. The same year that GUS purchased TRW from Tom Lee, TRW and CCN Group merged to form what is now known as Experian.

Experian's United States headquarters is in Costa Mesa, California. Its primary business is managing huge computer databases that store information on customer buying patterns and their credit history. Experian is paid each time a request is made for credit from a consumer. If there are more than two hundred million credit files stored in their database, how much do you think they are making a day from inquiries alone? Here is something else to think about: Experian is the fifteenth largest internet company in the world and owns LowerMyBills.com, the Home Shopping Network, Burberry, and Auto Check which gives title reports on automobiles that are being sold or accepted for trade. This system is used by more than 97% of auto dealers in the United States. Later I will explain why this is important when it comes to guarding your personal information.

TransUnion had a very interesting beginning, that dates back into the 1800s and John D. Rockefeller who owned Standard Oil. Standard controlled oil shipping because of its monopoly on all the tank cars in the United States. It was doing great until the government stepped in to regulate its hold on the railcar industry. After the government started creating problems for Standard Oil, it created the Union Tank Line Company a stand-alone corporation, in 1891. In 1911 the United States Supreme Court dissolved Standard Oil, making Union Tank Line an independent corporation.

In 1919 Union Tank Line amended its name to Union Tank Car Company and begin to be publicly traded on the New York Stock Exchange. Due to the nature of its business of leasing and selling oil tank cars and the possibility of profit loss, the company had to keep records on its customers.

Union Tank Car Company wanted its recordkeeping to be detailed, so they bought the Credit Bureau of Cook County in 1967. In 1968, Union Tank Car Company created TransUnion as its parent holding company. In 1972, it started a system that stored data on tapes and discs. In 1981, Union Tank Car Company sold TransUnion to the Marmon Group, a company that is privately owned by the Pritzkers of Chicago, Illinois during a time when the business was failing. The Marmon Group takes its name from the Marmon motor car that created the roadster that won the Indy 500 in 1911.

The Marmon Group was started in 1902 by Nicholas Pritzker. Today, the Pritzkers not only own TransUnion, they also own the Hyatt Hotel chain; Ticketmaster; Royal Caribbean Cruises; Accutronics; Hammond Organ Company; Pritzker Family Children's Zoo in Chicago; First Health Group; Nabisco: Elgin Grand Victoria Casino; Colson Corp; Pritzker Realty Group; and Pritzker Military Library. In 2004, the Pritzker family was number forty-seven on the list of the world's richest people.

Most people are familiar with Equifax simply because of good marketing and advertising. Equifax is the leader when it comes to credit reporting agencies. It was founded by Cator and Guy Woolford, two brothers from Chattanooga, Tennessee. Cator was part owner in a local grocery store and kept credit history on their customers. Mainly for the town's Retail Grocers' Association. In 1899, Cator talked his younger brother, Guy, into moving to Atlanta, Georgia, to start a business. Guy was an attorney, and at the time, his practice was not doing so well. Cator wanted to relocate to Atlanta because he saw opportunity there because of the population. That same year they started a business called Retail Credit Company.

In the beginning, they sold a merchants guide, which contained the credit records of many citizens who lived in the city. The first guide was sold to a department store called J.M. High Company. In 1901 Retail Credit Company discovered that more money could be made in the life insurance industry, since in 1901 insurance was associated with credit.

Retail Credit Company was incorporated in 1913, and by 1916, it was also involved in the mortgage business. During this time, there were major dollars being made in the insurance and mortgage businesses, and Retail Credit Company capitalized on those industries. In 1970, Congress passed the Fair Credit Reporting Act, setting limits on the data that credit bureaus could have on one person. That same year Retail Credit Company's credit files became automated.

In 1971, Retail Credit Company began trading on the New York Stock Exchange. During this time, it was discovered that Retail Credit Company had many errors contained within its recordkeeping. As a result, it changed its name to Equifax. Over the years Equifax has grown into a billion-dollar industry. In 1994, Equifax entered into a joint venture with Asociacion Nacional de Entidades de Financiacion to operate a Spanish credit reporting company. Equifax is a beast that has control of many insurance and healthcare entities.

This should be a warning to you as a consumer because it may be invading your privacy even when you are unaware. For years, Equifax and AT&T have been working on a sophisticated network allowing medical records to be accessed and downloaded by any doctor or specialist a person visits. Back in March 1995, Equifax and AT&T issued a press release stating they were joining to form its new Healthcare Information Services Group, a cluster of six businesses with more than fifty interrelated products and services. If this happens, they will control the nation's largest network repository of medical records.

Keep in mind that Equifax owns HealthChex Inc., Osborn

Laboratories, and Electronic Tabulating Services. Equifax and Lotus Development Corp are trying to put the names, addresses, and profiles of more than a hundred million consumers on a single CD-ROM. This system will enable a marketer to print up a mailing list of possibly every woman aged twenty-five to forty-five with a household income of more than $60,000 within a ten-mile radius.

Remember TransUnion owns First Health Group. The point I am trying to make is that this truly may be the mark of the beast. Equifax has been in the insurance business since 1901, and even today one of its biggest clients is FedEx, which contracts out its property damage data to a division of Equifax called Insurance Information Services. Not only does Equifax handle commercial clients, it runs huge databanks for the auto and home insurance industry. This databank is called CLUE, short for Comprehensive Loss Underwriting Exchange. This system tracks your auto accidents and claims on your homeowners insurance. Equifax also controls Choice Point, which is on the New York Stock Exchange.

Choice Point's database holds at least twenty billion social security numbers, credit and medical histories, motor vehicle registrations, job applications, lawsuits, criminal files, and professional licenses. Choice Point owns a DNA analysis lab and facilitates drug testing for employers, another way to gather sensitive information since when you take a drug test you must show your identification. If after reading this brief history on the credit bureaus, you cannot see the puzzle being formed, I suggest you do your own research. If you would like to invest in Equifax, contact:

Equifax
Christy Cooper
Investor Relations and Shareholder
404-885-8300

The fourth largest credit bureau which is hardly known is Innovis Data Solutions.It was formerly known as ABC Services. Founded in 1970 by Associated Credit Bureaus to provide consumer credit data to member affiliates the company was sold in 1989 and changed its name to Consumer Credit Associates. First Data Corporation purchased the company in 1997 and renamed it Innovis Data Solutions.

HOW CREDIT BUREAUS WORK

Credit bureaus are private for-profit companies that collect data on the credit history of people to then sell to the commercial and financial enterprises that extend credit. The bureaus get this information from many sources and consolidate it into one database that provides reports to different creditors to show all the credit history related to a particular person or company. Before the bureaus can collect any credit information, they must enter into an agreement with the different institutions that hold this data. These institutions are normally known as members or affiliate credit institutions.

These companies make an agreement with the credit bureaus to give them information about the credit history of their customers in return for having access to the credit bureaus' database known as E-OSCAR. The terms of the agreement usually state what information will be provided, the number of times per month it will be given, and the responsibility of each company to guarantee successful data transmission. The agreement also includes confidentiality clauses, data security, and payment for service. When the credit information comes into the credit bureaus' databases for the different companies, they all are updated by way of a nine-track tape or ribbon. This is simply an electronic update each month from the different companies. When updating, businesses use a digit code: 1-on time, 2-thirty days late, etc.

The software system E-OSCAR performs a quality check on the information, such as looking for format errors and data that does not correspond to the codes I mentioned earlier. Credit bureaus do not verify the content of the information they receive. The company sending the credit information usually does this. E-OSCAR is the heart of the credit bureaus. If you can understand it and the laws that govern it, you can basically control your credit file.

I have provided you with parts of a letter that was written by Ms. Jennifer J. Johnson, secretary for the Board of Governors of the Federal Reserve System, in which she speaks about the databases the bureaus use to maintain information.

"Generally, while the vast majority of disputes about information furnished to consumer reporting agencies are received directly from consumer reporting agencies rather than consumers, banks treat all disputes similarly, investigating promptly and within the Fair Credit Reporting Act timeframes. In many cases, the process of receiving disputes from consumer reporting agencies and responding is automated."

Later in the letter she states, "Banks rely on their own records to submit information in an automated fashion, using the codes, forms, and formats required by the consumer reporting agencies. The files (tapes) are then submitted to the consumer reporting agencies on a monthly basis and uploaded to their systems."

I put the last statement in bold because I wanted you to understand that almost every verification process that takes place between banks (credit card companies) is all done by codes and is automated. Remember earlier when I told you that creditors update their information on their customers by using what is called a ribbon? This is what Ms. Johnson is talking about in the sentence that I have in bold print. The system that the banks is uploading information to is known as E-OSCAR.

Ms. Johnson goes on to talk about the E-OSCAR system: "That system uses dispute type codes to identify the nature of the dispute in order to guide the furnisher in its investigation. After investigating, furnishers respond with the appropriate automated code, either verifying that the information is correct or providing corrected information." Remember everything is verified by automated codes. This means limited information is provided, which makes it hard for the consumer.

She adds, "The E-OSCAR system has the advantage of expediting the dispute process so that furnishers and consumer reporting agencies can comply with the tight deadlines of Fair Credit Reporting Act. By nature an automated system means less can be transmitted and considered. In some cases, the dispute codes lack sufficient specificity of the nature of the dispute, sometimes because the consumer has provided insufficient information. In those cases, the furnisher relies on its own internal data information and process to investigate."

Notice the words in bold. This very statement is usually what happens when you, the consumer, try to take the traditional route of questioning incorrect accounts on your credit report. I am sure almost every person who has tried to dispute inaccurate information on his or her credit report has received a letter from the credit bureau stating, "The account information has been verified as belonging to you." That is because the agencies are relying on their own internal system. This is why you must find a way to outsmart the credit bureaus.

YOUR ZIP CODE CAN HURT YOUR CREDIT RATING

All credit bureaus have a system they use to ensure that extending someone credit will not come back to haunt them. Pay attention to the geographic code used in the form I've included. These codes help the credit bureaus and creditors diagnose how well you will pay your bills, depending on in which part of town you live. Through these geographic zip codes creditors or credit bureaus can distinguish whether you live in a low-income neighborhood, a middle-class, or a very affluent part of town. They will also be able to distinguish the statistics on how likely you are to become delinquent on your bills or file bankruptcy. This may sound like a conspiracy theory to some, but believe me when I tell you that their method is very real. The credit bureaus make money off your bad credit, not the good credit. They are in the business of selling your personal information to those companies who are willing to pay.

Personal Information

The following information is reported to us by you, your creditors and other sources. Each source may report your personal information differently, which may result in variations of your name, address, Social Security number, etc. As part of our fraud-prevention program, a notice with additional information may appear.

Names

Telephone numbers

Spouse's first name

Employers

Notices

Residences

The geographical code shown with each address identifies the state, county, census tract, block group and Metropolitan Statistical Area associated with each address.

Address	Type of address	Geographical
	Single family	57-4920
	Post office box 0-21	20
	Apartment 0-2	0
	Single family	0-00
	Single family	0-20

Social Security number variations
As a security precaution, we did not list the Social Security number that you gave us when you contacted us.
Date of birth

Telephone numbers

HOW CREDIT REPORTS WORK

Credit scoring is a scientific method that uses statistical models to assess an individual's creditworthiness based on credit history and current credit accounts. Credit scoring was first developed in the 1950s, but has come into increasing use in just the last two decades.

In the early 1980s the three major credit bureaus, Equifax, Experian, and TransUnion all worked with the Fair Isaac Corporation to develop generic scoring models that allow each bureau to offer a score based solely on the contents of the credit bureau's data about an individual.

Each credit bureau has its own unique system however the scoring models have been normalized so that a numerical score at one bureau is the equivalent of the same numerical score at another. Thus, a score of 700 from Equifax indicates the same creditworthiness as a score of 700 from TransUnion or Experian, even though the calculations used to determine those scores are different at each bureau.

Creditors especially in the mortgage industry frequently use these scores known as FICO scores as an important factor in the decision whether to offer credit. The scores range from 350 to 850 points, but those numbers mean little on their own. They become meaningful and useful within the context of a particular lender's own cutoff points and underwriting guidelines.

In general, you are likely to be considered a better credit risk if your FICO score is high. Under mortgage lending guidelines, for example, a score of 650 or above indicates a very good credit history. People with these scores will usually find obtaining credit quick and easy and will have a good chance to get it on favorable terms.

Scores between 620 and 650 (average FICO scores fall into this range) indicate basically good credit, but also suggest to lenders that they should look at the potential borrower to assess any particular credit risks before extending a large loan or high credit limit. People with scores in this range have a good chance at obtaining credit at a good rate, but may have to provide additional documentation and explanations to the lender before a large loan is approved. This means that their loan closing may take longer, making their experience more like that of borrowers in the days before credit scoring, when every individual was researched.

A score below 620 may prevent a borrower from getting the best interest rates, as they may be considered a greater credit risk but it does not mean that they can't get credit. The process will probably be lengthier and, as noted, the terms may be less appealing, but often credit can still be obtained.

Also informative is the list of reasons that may be provided to account for why a score isn't higher. With each credit score generated, the credit bureau also creates a list of the four most significant reasons either for a poor score or, in the case of a good score, for why it isn't "perfect."

The possible FICO reasons are:
- Amount owed on accounts is too high.
- Delinquency on accounts.

- Too few bank revolving accounts.
- Too many bank or national revolving accounts.
- Too many accounts with balances.
- Consumer finance accounts.
- Account payment history too new to rate.
- Too many recent inquiries in the last twelve months.
- Too many accounts opened in the last twelve months.
- Proportion of balances to credit limits is too high on revolving accounts.
- Amount owed on revolving accounts is too high.
- Length of revolving credit history is too short.
- Time since delinquency is too recent or unknown.
- Length of credit history is too short.
- Lack of recent bank revolving information.
- Lack of recent revolving account information.
- No recent non-mortgage balance information.
- Number of accounts with delinquency.
- Too few accounts currently paid as agreed.
- Time since derogatory public record or collection.
- Amount past due on accounts.
- Serious delinquency, derogatory public record, or collection.
- Too many bank or national revolving accounts with balances.
- No recent revolving balances.
- Proportion of loan balances to loan amounts is too high.
- Lack of recent installment loan information.
- Date of last inquiry too recent.
- Time since most recent account opening too short.
- Number of revolving accounts.
- Number of bank revolving or other revolving accounts.
- Number of established accounts.
- Number of recent bankcard balances.
- Too few accounts with recent payment information.

People have become increasingly dependent on credit. Therefore, it's crucial that you understand personal credit reports and your credit rating (or score). Here we'll explore what a credit score is, how it is determined, why it is important, and some tips to acquire and maintain good credit.

When you use credit, you are borrowing money that you promise to pay back within a specified period of time. A credit score is a statistical method to determine the likelihood of an individual paying back the money he or she has borrowed.

The credit bureaus that issue these scores have different evaluation systems, each based on different factors. Some may take into consideration only the information contained in your credit report. The primary factors used to calculate an individual's credit score are credit payment history, current debts, length of credit history, and frequency of applications for new credit.

You may hear the term FICO score in reference to your credit score - the terms are essentially synonymous. FICO is an acronym for the Fair Isaacs Corporation, the creator of the software used to calculate credit scores.

Scores range between 350 (extremely high risk) and 850 (extremely low risk). Below is a breakdown of the distribution of scores for the American population in 2003.

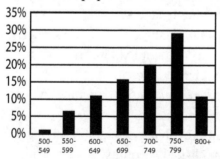

WHAT ABOUT A CREDIT RATING?

In addition to using credit (FICO) scores, most countries (including the United States and Canada) use a scale of 09 to rate your personal credit. On this scale, each number is preceded by one of two letters: "I" signifies installment credit (like home or auto financing), and "R" stands for revolving credit (such as a credit card).

Each creditor will issue its own rating for individuals. For example, you may have an R1 rating with Visa (the highest level of credit rating), but you might simultaneously have an R5 from MasterCard if you've neglected to pay your MasterCard bill for many months. Although the "R" and "I" systems are still in use, the prevailing trend is to move away from this multiple rating scale toward the single-digit FICO score. Nevertheless, here is how the scale breaks down:

- **R0 or I0** You are new to the credit world, and you have an insufficient credit history for making an accurate judgment of your future risk.
- **R1 or I1** You pay your credit back in one month.
- **R2 or I2** You pay your credit back in two months.
- **R3 or I3** You pay your credit back in three months.
- **R4 pr I4** You pay your credit back in four months.
- **R5 or I5** You have not repaid in four months, but you are not a "9" yet.
- **R7 or I7** Your debt payments are made under consolidation.
- **R8 or I8** Debt was cleared by selling the item (repossession).
- **R9 or I9** You officially have bad debt default, which usually means it is not collectible.

WHAT MAKES UP YOUR CREDIT SCORE?

When you borrow money your lender sends information to a credit bureau that details, in the form of a credit report, how well you handled your debt. From the information in the credit report, the bureau determines a credit score based on five major factors:

1. Previous credit performance

2. Current level of indebtedness
3. Time credit has been in use
4. Types of credit available
5. Pursuit of new credit.

Although all these factors are included in credit score calculations, they are not given equal weighting. The pie chart below shows how things break down:

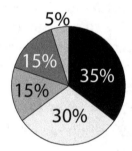

35% – Pervious Credit Performance
30% – Current Level of Indedtedness
15% – Time Credit has been in use
15% – Types of Credit Available
5% – Pursuit of New Credit

As you can see by the pie graph, your credit rating is most affected by your historical propensity for paying off your debt. The factor that can boost your credit rating the most is having a past that shows you pay off your debts fairly quickly. Additionally, maintaining low levels of indebtedness (or not keeping huge balances on your credit cards or other lines of credit) having a long credit history, and refraining from constantly applying for additional credit will all help your credit score.

Although I would love to explain the exact formula for calculating the credit score, the Federal Trade Commission has a secretive approach to this formula.

WHY YOUR CREDIT RATING IS IMPORTANT.

When you apply for a credit card, mortgage, or even phone service, your credit rating is checked. Credit reports make it possible for stores to accept checks, banks to issue credit or debit cards, and corporations to manage their operations. Depending on your credit score, lenders determine what risk you pose to them.

The table below shows how individuals with varying credit scores will pay dramatically different interest rates on similar mortgage amounts the difference in interest, in turn, has a large impact on the monthly payments which pay off both interest and principal:

Score	Rate	Monthly Payment
720-850	5.49%	$851
700-719	5.61%	$862
675-699	6.15%	$914
620-674	7.30%	$1,028
560-619	8.53%	$1,157
500-559	9.29%	$1,238

CREDIT BUREAU COMPUTER SYSTEMS

Credit bureaus were originally meant for the purpose of providing a financial profile of a potential consumer to a lender. Now, credit bureaus are used by everyone from landlords to database vendors. The relationship between credit bureau financial data with information provided to them by banks, mortgage companies, marketers, and credit card companies has made anyone seeking credit vulnerable to one of the most powerful database systems in the world. This database system is held by the credit bureaus.

People today do not realize the relationship between database vendors and even the smallest entities such as grocery stores. Some grocery stores offer you what they call a plus card. This card supposedly gives you a discount on the things you purchase, but in actuality it captures and stores information about you such as the type of items you buy. This may be small peanuts to some people, but it is major league to others. This is merely something to think about the next time you are in a grocery store and you are asked, if you are interested in a plus or discount card.

When you fill out the application for a discount card or even a warranty card, this is a way of collecting private information that may be used by direct marketer databases. Direct marketers and insurance companies can buy your information so they can make you credit card offers. If they can buy it, that makes for good business even to a small grocery store chain.

Many people do not understand how easy it is to get personal information on anybody. For instance, the Federal Trade Commission has a website called EDGAR. On this site you can obtain Social Security numbers for millions of people who have disclosed this information on different forms and filings. Think about whom the Federal Trade Commission is supposed to govern. (Hint: the credit bureaus.)

If a bank made the names, addresses, date of birth, and Social Security numbers of all its customers available to the public, there would be a major issue. This, in reality, is exactly what the credit bureaus are doing for anyone who is willing to pay.

Below are a few addresses and websites that are made available to companies or individuals seeking to gain personal information on anyone they choose.

Lexis-Nexis
P.O. Box 933
Dayton, Ohio 45401-0933
http://www.lexisnexis.com

Information Resource Service Company
3777 N. Harbor Blvd.
Fullerton, California 92835
http://www.irsc.com
USA Datalink
6711 Bayway Drive

Baytown, TX 77520
www.usadatalink.com

ACME Information
164 Manningham Drive
Madison, AL 35758
http://iquest.com/~leahwes/ACMEInf.htm

HOW CREDIT BUREAUS ESTABLISH YOUR FILE

The credit bureaus have a database designed to retrieve files that allow them to identify each consumer. The system is mandatory because each credit file has to be separate, even when the names and addresses are similar. The problem with this is, none of the credit bureaus has come up with a perfect system. That is why you will quite often see information on your credit file that belongs to someone else who may have similar information. The credit bureaus try to maintain accurate records, but this is almost impossible. Equifax and Experian have two types of files on each individual. This is done so that credit files cannot be merged. They use what is called a type A system. TransUnion also uses what is called a type B system that is established mainly on the consumer's Social Security number, employer identification number (EIN), or taxpayer identification number (TIN). If the consumer's name, address, and zip code do not match the last four digits of the Social Security number that is stored in the database, then a new file is created. You will understand why this is a problem for the credit bureaus later in the book.

The type A system that Equifax and Experian use allow consumers' identifying information to be entered into the computer system in an attempt to match existing data. If no matching information is found, a new file is created. The credit bureaus' computer systems are very sophisticated but simple. Their matching system is designed in the following format:

1. **LAST NAME**—The computer only identifies the first ten letters of the last name. Letters must match an existing file, or a new file will be created and the computer will stop the search. If a match is made, the computer will proceed.
2. **FIRST NAME**—If the last name matches an existing file, the computer will continue by searching for the first three letters of the first name. If the first name matches an existing file, the system will then proceed to match other identifying information.
3. **MIDDLE INITIAL**—After the first and last names have been matched, the computer will check for the middle initial. If it finds a match, it will continue.
4. **SPOUSE**—If a person is married, the spouse's first initial will appear after the file holder's middle initial. If the person is not married, the computer will try to match other identifying information.
5. **NUMERIC ADDRESS**—When all the above information matches, the computer will try to match the first five digits of the numeric address.
6. **STREET NAME**—The computer will match the numeric address with the first letter of the street.
7. **ZIP CODE**—The computer will match the address that is retrieved with zip code. If the consumer has been at the address more than three years, the computer will stop. A search showing other people with similar names and addresses will cause the computer to merge the files, and a flag will be added to it.
8. **PREVIOUS ADDRESS**—If the consumer has not lived at the residence longer than three years, the computer will check previous addresses. The credit bureaus' computer system can hold up to ten previous addresses, but will usually list only the last three.
9. **DATE OF BIRTH**—The system will match the consumer's year of birth only.

10. **SOCIAL SECURITY NUMBER**—The computer will match all the previous identifying information with the last four digits of the consumer's Social Security number. If the number does not match the previous reported number, a flag will be added to the consumer's credit file. The credit bureaus also maintain files on employer identification numbers (EIN) and taxpayer identification numbers (TIN).

If you are wondering if the following information is accurate, here is something to consider. When you call to request a copy of your credit report, take note of all the identifying information the automated computer system requests from you then think about the information that is required when you go to fill out a credit application. The credit bureaus need all of the other identifying factors such as your name, address, and date of birth because they are not authorized to use your full Social Security number for the purpose of establishing a credit file. Because you give them so much information when you fill out a credit application, it is easy for the computer system to use the previously described method. If the credit bureaus were authorized to use your Social Security number to establish your credit file they would have access to more than the last four digits of your Social Security number when searching the pacer system for those individuals who have filed bankruptcy.

Your Social Security number was created during the Great Depression for the purpose of establishing basically a savings account for individuals to retain after retirement however, it has turned into something more than just a savings account number, and part of that is because that bank (Social Security) is broke.

WAYS TO OUTSMART CREDIT BUREAUS

There are many ways of outsmarting the credit bureaus. I am in no way instructing anyone to practice these methods, but I thought I would share a few of them because they are simple, clever techniques at least one individual used to repair his entire credit report. As a child, do you recall forging your mom or dad's signature on a report card or a doctor's excuse for school? Well, it is almost like that in a sense. You simply send the credit card company certain bogus information so that the company will respond to you in writing. Once you have a copy of the company's letterhead, you cut and paste your information so it looks like the letter was addressed to you.

Make up a name or Social Security number, and using your own address contact the creditor. They will respond with a letter on their own letterhead. Your next step is very easy. Replace the name, Social Security number and other relevant information with your own.

After, you have scanned or cut and pasted all of this new information, send a copy of the new letter to the three major credit bureaus. They will automatically delete the accounts from your credit file without questioning or verification from the creditor. Why don't they verify, you may be asking? There are more than two hundred million credit files in the credit bureaus' data system. Do you think they have time to verify information on each file or every dispute?

Remember earlier when I told you that the verification process used by the credit bureaus and creditors is done by way of E-OSCAR. That means there is a number code being used to verify information, but if you are sending them documentation from the creditor, there is no need for them to verify this information.

The thing about credit bureaus is that they never let their right hand know what their left hand is doing. What I mean by this is that the credit bureaus are divided into different departments, and one may not know or understand what the other is doing.

The irony of all these departments is that one will delete something that another won't. For example, the consumer relations department will tell you they can't delete a fraudulent account. Another department may even send you a letter saying, "We were unable to authenticate the copy of the identity theft report that you sent us; therefore, we are unable to process your request to block information. However, if you provide specific information, we are investigating the information you questioned with the sources." Do not fall for this trick being used by the credit bureaus. They simply are trying to discourage you from sending information that allows you to remove items from your credit report.

The thing that some customer service agents who work in the consumer relations department do not know is that if you send a police report stating that the item you are disputing is bogus, by law, the Fraud Victim Assistance department will automatically delete the account you claim to be fraudulent. The beautiful thing about this is that it doesn't matter if the creditor responds and says that the disputed item is yours or that it is not fraud.

The Fair and Accurate Credit Transaction Act states that the item must be deleted if it is accompanied by a police report. The FACT Act also establishes national requirements for data blocking and requires that within four business days from receiving a police report, credit bureaus must block any information in a consumer's credit file that resulted from an alleged identity theft. The credit bureaus will tell you they have up to thirty days to investigate the information you are disputing. This simply is not true.

The FACT Act places these requirements relating to blocked information on the credit bureaus, but it also has requirements for data furnishers. If the data furnisher aka creditor receives a notice that a specific account has been blocked, the creditor may not provide the account information to any credit bureau. Since the credit bureaus have blocked the information, the consumer no longer has a relationship with the creditor. Therefore, the bureaus cannot supply any information relating to a blocked account to a creditor. The creditor doesn't even have the right to pull the consumer's credit file anymore because it no longer has a permissible purpose to access this information.

Not only that, remember that credit bureaus are also governered by the Consumer Data Industry Association, better known as E-OSCAR.

When it comes to fraudulent information on a consumer's credit report E-Oscar guidelines state, "If a consumer submits an identity theft report to a furnisher and states that information maintained by the furnisher resulted from identity theft, the furnisher may not provide the information to any bureau, unless the furnisher subsequently determines or is informed by the consumer that the information is correct." Notice the part of this section that I have put in bold. The consumer, you has to inform them that the information being reported is correct.

Another rule that relates to fraudulent information is that

blocked data due to a police report cannot be sold. E-OSCAR states, "No person shall sell, transfer, or place for collection a debt that such person has been notified has been blocked by a nationwide credit bureau." What that means is that once you send a police report in to the credit bureaus and they delete the fraudulent information, the creditor cannot sell the account or turn it over to a collection agency.

If you are concerned about the information you have claimed as fraud ever being replaced on your credit don't worry. E-OSCAR states, "A data furnisher must have reasonable procedures to respond to any notification that it receives from a credit bureau pursuant to the trade line blocking provisions to prevent the furnisher from refurnishing the blocked information." What all this means is that the creditor has to make sure that the information that has been deleted from your credit file does not show up again.

It may not have occurred to you that there is a reason why the credit bureaus have different departments and why their employees have limited knowledge about what the other departments are doing. Think about it: if the credit bureaus allowed their customer service agents to understand and know everything that is going on, the agents could easily do plenty of damage to the credit bureaus as well as helping themselves in the process. This is the reason you must be aggressive when trying to restore your credit. What I mean by this is that you should not just deal with one department. You should always take notes when speaking to someone from the credit bureaus as well as pay close attention to the things they tell you as it relates to your credit.

There is always someone sleeping or slipping on the job, and that person may very well give you the information you need. Overall, credit bureaus not only seek to give you, the consumer, a hard time. They also seek to keep their employees in the dark about the entire inner workings simply because this is their way of protecting themselves. The bureaus train their employees to keep consumer calls under four minutes. The problem with this is you are considered a consumer and not a customer.

In 2000, Equifax, TransUnion, and Experian agreed to pay a total of $2.5 million to settle allegations by the Federal Trade Commission that they violated the Fair Credit Reporting Act by failing to maintain adequate staffing for their toll-free telephone numbers. The Federal Trade Commission said the companies "blocked millions of calls from consumers who wanted to discuss the contents and possible errors in their credit reports and kept some of those consumers on hold for unreasonably long periods of time."

Keep in mind that if they speak with you, you have four minutes to state your claim. In 2003, the issue resurfaced when Equifax agreed to pay $250,000 to settle FTC allegations that its blocked-call rate and hold times violated the 2000 consent decree.

The credit bureaus do not consider the people they maintain credit data on as customers. These individuals are considered to be consumers. The true customers are the banks, insurance companies, credit card companies, or any businesses willing to pay for your personal information. Think about this statement made by Mr. Davis, a consumer credit executive who formerly worked at TransUnion: "During the fifteen years I was involved, there was no doubt that the credit bureaus' customers were the creditors. They didn't want to consider the consumer as a customer because they were viewed as an expense. Every time there was a consumer who knocked on the door, we weren't getting any money from them." This information lets you know that the credit bureaus are in the business to make money, and you, the consumer, do not fall under that old cliché "the customer is always right."

KEEPING TRACK OF YOUR CREDIT

Some people do not realize how important it is to read the fine print when they are filling out credit card applications. The reason why this practice is so important is because a bank guarantees each credit card for which you apply. Once you find one company that extends you credit, you should pay attention to what bank is guaranteeing the card because, if it has approved you for one card that means that you probably qualify for others it guarantees for other companies. They may have a point system set up like the one described below.

- "Mark 12 points"
- Age-Mark is 33 years old, thus a grade of 0.
- Martial status-Mark is single, for a grade of 0.
- Plus-Mark does have a home phone grade 0.
- Number of Dependents-Mark has no children, thus 0.
- Residence-Mark rents an apartment. He's lived there for six years, +2.
- Time on Job-Mark has also been employed for six years in the same job, +2.
- Type of Employment-Mark is a cab driver, for a grade of -3.
- Spouse's employment-this question does not apply to Mark, as he is single.
- Income weekly-Mark earns $250 per week.
- Income Monthly-Mark earns over $1,000 per month, I 3.
- Annual Income-Mark earns over $12,000 annually, I 3.
- Monthly Obligations-Mark's car payment is $265 per month, -2.
- Credit History-Mark was late twice on his car payment, -2.

Based on Mark's past performance in all these categories, he received a score of +3. This is a high enough score to grant him credit.

A much simpler point system that is sometimes used by lenders and credit grantors is set up by using five simple requirements: a salary of a least $1,500 per month, at least five years at present address, employed at present job for at least two years, a paying-on-time credit history with no late payments, and a telephone in your name.

All three credit bureaus maintain a scoring system based on the format that is shown below.

Consumer Credit Score

Name: **File Number:**
Address: **Date of Credit Score:**

About your credit score:

A credit score is a computer generated mathematical calculation of the information which appears in a credit report. It represents your credit worthiness as a number or a numerical value. The credit score is based on data about your credit history and payment behavior. Credit scores are used to assist a lender or insurance company in determining the level of risk associated with granting you a loan, or evaluating an insurance policy. Credit scores can change over time, depending on how your credit history and payment behavior changes and how well you manage your credit obligations.

Since the credit score is based on information in your credit history, it is important that you review the credit report that is being furnished with this document to make sure it is complete and accurate.

The credit score, displayed below, is created by   A higher credit score means a lower likelihood of delinquency in the next two years on a new account. The credit score is presented with up to four key factors. These factors will print in the order of importance as to the reasons your credit score is not higher. Use these as a guide for how to improve your   credit score.

Please note that this credit score may be different than a credit score used by a lending institution or insurance company. The credit industry and the insurance industry use many different types of credit scores. For more information, visit

Factor 1: Collection amounts ever owed are too high:

Consumers with collection activity are more likely of future delinquency. Making prompt payments over a longer period of time may improve your score.

Factor 2: Too many serious delinquencies:

Your credit report reflects one or more accounts with a delinquent payment history of 90 days or more delinquent. Making prompt payments over time may improve your credit score.

Factor 3: Months since most recent serious delinquency is too short:

Your credit report reflects a delinquent payment history. Making prompt payments over time may improve your credit score.

Factor 4: Too few satisfactory revolving accounts:

The number of good standing revolving accounts is too low.

How to Outsmart the Credit Bureaus

GETTING STARTED

The first step to improving your credit is ordering your reports. You can get them by calling the following companies:

Equifax: 888-685-1111

Experian: 888-397-3742

TransUnion: 800-888-4213

The next step is taking your name off prescreened offers for different credit cards or insurance offers. These are those unsolicited offers you receive in the mail that say you have been preapproved. Most of them are not worth the paper on which they are printed. This can be done by logging on to www.optoutprescreen.com or calling 888-567-8688. You can also write to the credit bureaus at the following addresses to opt-out.

Options
Equifax, Inc.
P.O. Box 740123
Atlanta, GA 30374-0123

Experian
Consumer Opt-Out
701 Experian Parkway
Allen, TX 75013

TransUnion Corporation
Name Removal Option
P.O. Box 97328
Jackson, MS 39288-7328

TransUnion Corporation
Name Removal Option
P.O. Box 505
Woodlyn, PA 19094

Use the following sample letter when contacting the credit bureaus:

Date
Name
Address
City, State, Zip

To Whom It May Concern:
I request to have my name removed from your marketing lists. Thank you for your prompt attention to my request.

Sincerely,
Your signature
Your name

I have often heard of people complaining about not being able to get their credit report even after contacting the bureaus. If you are one of those individuals who has been told, "We are unable to process your request with the information you have provided, please send a copy of your driver's license and Social Security card," do not send the credit bureaus any copies of any information relating to your identity. It may come back to hurt you in ways you would not believe.

If you've been denied a credit report, the first thing you want to do is apply for credit at three different stores. They can be department stores or, jewelry stores, or even a major credit card over the phone. Do not worry about being turned down because that is not the reason for applying. Whether you are approved or not, the inquiry will instantly register in the credit bureaus' databases, which do not know whether you were denied or approved. When you call the toll-free numbers again, you should have no problem getting a copy of your credit report at no cost.

Please remember that by law you are entitled to one free copy of your credit report annually from each bureau. If you are ever denied utility service or asked to pay a deposit, you can get payment information from Equifax Utilities and Telecommunications by calling: 888-201-5643.

After, you receive your credit reports, make multiple copies of the dispute forms that come with them so that you have them on hand while removing items from your credit file. The next thing you should do is find all the items on the credit report that are inaccurate. Pay special attention to accounts that do not belong to you because they will serve a great purpose in removing items off your credit report. I will explain this in greater detail in the section entitled "Fighting Identity Theft."

There may be times when you cannot get a copy of your credit report even after you have taken the steps previously mentioned. This is not a problem. What has probably happened is that there are multiple addresses on your credit report or there is no file listed for you under the name and address you have provided. If this happens, call the following numbers listed for each credit bureau. You will get a live voice. Explain what your problem is as it relates to getting your credit report.

Equifax: 404-885-8000
Experian: 714-830-5220
TransUnion: 610-546-460

REMOVING BANKRUPTCY FROM YOUR CREDIT

Removing bankruptcy may seem difficult to do, but it has been done. Remember that the described procedures are illegal and may be punishable by law.

The scan or cut-and-paste method can be used with bankruptcies and other public records. Credit bureaus verify civil judgments and other public records besides bankruptcies with the name and address only. A simple way for you to use the cut-and-paste method with public records is to replace your Social Security number with a made- up one or a different address and send a copy of that information to the credit bureaus. Once the credit bureaus notice the inaccuracies you have outlined for them, they will automatically delete the information from your credit file since it is considered inaccurate.

This can also be done with bankruptcy petitions. The credit bureaus will lie to you and say that the federal bankruptcy courts have placed the bankruptcy on your credit file and that it cannot be removed. The truth is the federal bankruptcy courts in no way report to the credit bureaus nor do they act in conjunction with them. Each of the three major credit bureaus have what they call agents who work for outside companies to check a pacer system every day to see who has filed bankruptcy. The web address of this pacer system is http://pacer.psc.uscourts.gov and the phone number is 800-676-6856. Once they pull this information from the pacer system, the computer system matches the first name with the last, numeric address with zip code, and most importantly the last four digits of the individual's Social Security number. They also use a third-party database company called Lexis-Nexis. This company specializes in public records. To obtain a copy of your Lexis-Nexis report, make a request by mail:

Lexis-Nexis,
100 S. Fifth Avenue, Suite 300
Minneapolis, MN 55402

The credit bureaus also only have access to the last four digits of your Social Security number when it comes to bankruptcies. This little piece of information in itself is just what you need to find a discrepancy to use against the credit bureaus. How do you use these discrepancies? Well, you simply send a letter to them and cut and paste a different address, zip code, or date of birth on the beginning part of your the Social Security number. Just in case you do not know how to obtain a copy of your bankruptcy petition or that of someone who has the same last name, you can use the pacer system to download a copy and print the bankruptcy petition of anyone just by typing his or her first and last name. Now, there are some individuals who may be skeptical or just do not believe this method will work. I say to these people, this information came directly from one of the credit bureaus' own. There may even be some individuals who think the credit bureaus will verify this information, but remember there are more than two hundred million credit files. Do you seriously believe they have time to verify, call, or investigate some, a few, or any disputable documents that are sent to them bearing what looks to be the letterhead of any creditor, civil, or bankruptcy court?

I am not advising anyone to attempt this method. One thing that I was told by one credit bureau employee was that the individual who did this made sure that when performing all of these steps, everything appeared to be uniform. He made sure that all of the font sizes and lettering were the same as the rest of the document he sent to the credit bureaus since they look for inconsistencies when they do receive documentation.

REMOVING INQUIRIES

There are two types of inquiries: soft and hard. Soft inquiries do not hurt your credit. Hard inquiries can remain on your credit report for up to two years and can affect your score dramatically. Hard inquiries typically occur when you apply for credit. The national average for credit inquiries by consumers is just three a year. When more than three inquiries a year appear on your credit report it look as though you are trying to hard to be approved for credit. There have been many questions about whether inquiries can be removed from your credit report, but no one has ever given a clear answer concerning this matter. Let me just say that the answer is yes. The easiest way to remove inquiries on your

Experian and Equifax credit report is simply disputing them by phone. Each time you dispute anything on your credit report, you are provided with a confirmation number and a phone number to contact the bureaus. Quite frankly, the best way to maintain your credit score even when you are obtaining new credit is to simply remove the inquiry before the newly acquired account shows up on your credit report. This can be done by disputing the inquiry as being yours.

When you contact the bureaus regarding your credit report, you simply dispute the inquiries on your file by stating that they do not belong to you or you do not remember applying for credit with the inquiry in question. The representative will more than likely ask you this infamous question: Do you think these inquiries are fraudulent? I am not instructing you to lie, but be creative with your response. TransUnion is the hardest credit bureau with which to deal despite whatever you may have read. I can honestly say that it is more difficult to have items removed from an Equifax and Experian report than TransUnion.

I had the opportunity to talk with a TransUnion employee. He described a method one individual used to remove inquiries from his credit report. Remember, I am in no way instructing anyone to perform this method because it is illegal. The man contacted TransUnion and requested the company send a list of all the creditors who had pulled his credit file. He made sure he told the representative to include the telephone numbers and addresses of each creditor. Once he was sent the list, he sent each creditor a letter stating he did not authorize the inquiries. Most of the creditors did not have a record of the credit applications since they were not authorized. The man didn't include his date of birth or Social Security number in the letter, which made it more difficult for the creditor even if his name was stored in the company's computer system. Once the creditor sent him a response stating there was no record reflecting the man had applied for credit with their company, he sent a copy of this letter by certified mail to TransUnion.

Another way of removing inquiries from your credit report if you have been a victim of identity theft or you suspect you have been a victim is to simply send a copy of your police report along with a list of the inquiries that don't belong to you or inquiries you did not authorize. You will only have to use this procedure with TransUnion because they will not dispute inquiries if you call. TransUnion will usually send you a letter like the one shown on the next page. Equifax and Experian will send you similar letters if you try to dispute inquiries by mail.

RETURN SERVICE REQUESTED

MARCH 25, 2005   FILE NUMBER

Thank you for contacting ▓▓▓▓▓▓▓▓. Our goal is to maintain
complete and accurate information on consumer credit reports. We
have provided the information below in response to your request.

Re: Explanation of Different Items on Your Credit Report

The inquiries listed on your credit report are a record of the
companies that obtained your credit information. All inquiries
remain on your credit report for two years. Credit information
will be provided only for the following permissible purposes:
credit transactions, employment consideration, review or
collection of an account, insurance underwriting, government
licensing, rental dwelling, or a response to a court order. Your
written authorization may not be required to constitute
permissible purpose. You may refer to the federal Fair Credit
Reporting Act for more information regarding permissible purpose.

If you believe that an inquiry on your credit report was made
without a permissible purpose, then you may wish to contact the
creditor directly.

The consumer disclosure (consum discl) inquiry refers to
▓▓▓▓▓▓▓▓ accessing your credit report. These inquiries are seen
only by you and ▓▓▓▓▓▓▓▓.

Re: General Policy

The federal Fair Credit Reporting Act requires ▓▓▓▓▓▓▓▓ to
investigate, free of charge, information on your credit report
that you believe is inaccurate, when you contact us directly with
your dispute. Some consumers use the services of credit repair
companies or "credit clinics" to submit disputes on the
consumer's behalf. The activities of these companies are
regulated by the Federal Credit Repair Organizations Act, and in
some states, by other laws.

REMOVING STUDENT LOANS

People often wonder if student loans can be removed from a personal credit file. The answer is yes. There are two ways student loans can be removed. One is legal: the other is not. Remember that the second one should not be attempted because it is illegal. Most people have the misconception that student loans are strictly the government. This is not true. When you take out a student loan, you are borrowing money from a financial institution that is granting you the loan based on the fact that if you do not pay it back, then the government will.

Now, let us examine this whole scenario of student loans. You go to school and take out one. If you get a degree you can't use or you can't find a job, you can't pay back the money you borrowed, and the lending institution is going to ruin your credit by reporting late or no payments on your student loans. The government is going to take your tax returns for the rest of your life because that is how long it is going to take you to pay them back. That is the down side of student loans.

The positive side is that you can file a police report claiming fraud on your student loan and it will automatically be blocked from your credit file. This is the illegal way. Legally, if you are disabled and can no longer work, you can file a petition to have your student loans automatically forgiven or wait twenty-six years and have your loans forgiven.

Student loans are not completely bad, if you can tap into your ability to think differently from those individuals whom I label as usual thinking people. If you have bad credit, student loans are the best type to receive. The reason I say this, is because they are guaranteed, no matter what your credit score looks like. If you decide to take out a student loan, the thing you must remember is be smart. Take the loan money and invest it into something like rental or cheap foreclosed properties. Maybe you can even start your own business. The possibilities are endless.

REMOVING INFORMATION THAT CAN HARM YOU

There are little things you should do when trying to improve your credit. It may seem small to you, but it will be very important when applying for credit. You want to always have mistakes and other people's information on your report removed because credit bureaus use this to verify who you are, and disputing it makes it easier when you try to remove negative items on your credit report because the credit bureaus no longer have this information to use against you.

You should also have all your past addresses as well as insignificant employment history deleted. At the most you should only have your present address showing on your credit report. This will show creditors that you are at least stable and you do not move around from place to place. You also want to delete extra phone numbers or duplicate variations of your name. Remember that credit bureaus collect as much information as they can on you because they are paid to do so, so try not to give them information such as a copy of your driver's license or Social Security card. The key thing to remember is that your credit is a reflection of you and your habits. Credit bureaus will tell you that it is against the law to knowingly dispute accurate information on your report and that it is punishable by law. This simply is not true. If you do not believe me, contact your attorney general's office. You can dispute any information on your credit report, even if you believe it is correct. One major way you can stop bill collectors from finding you to serve you civil warrants or send countless numbers of billing statements is to stop using your home address when filing your income tax returns. You can use a P.O. Box. Companies use skip tracers to track you down any way they can, and finding out where your last tax return was sent is the best way. Always try to keep your phone number private and use a P.O. Box as your mailing address. The reason I stress the importance of acquiring a private number is because creditors are like repossession agents. They sometimes will comb the telephone directory for the city in which you reside. They will then contact everyone with your last name until they find you.

By law, credit bureaus cannot disclose medical information relating to mental, physical, or behavioral health condition. Credit bureaus do not generally collect such information, but it could appear in the name of a data furnisher who reports your payment history to the credit bureaus. These names display in your credit report, but in reports to others they will display only as a medical payment. Given this information, that makes medical bills the easiest items on your credit to remove, if you dispute them as fraudulent. Some other items that are easy to remove are charge-offs, late payments, inquiries, repossessed items, bankruptcies that have been discharged, accounts that have been paid off that were bad accounts because you were late, and items that are more than three years old.

One of the reasons these items are so easy to remove is because most creditors do not even keep a hard copy of them and nine-times-out-of-ten, they will not be able to find relevant information on the item because most of it is only stored on a computer system, which is not good enough once it comes to producing hard copies to the credit bureaus when you dispute them. The creditor simply will not take the time to verify these outdated or unpaid items.

New consumer credit laws were passed to protect medical information. The Fair and Accurate Credit Transaction Act (FACT), signed by President Bush on December 4, 2003 (Public Law 108-159), establishes medical privacy provisions as part of consumer credit law. The bill amends the Fair Credit Reporting Act to include improved medical privacy protection, in addition to new protection against identity theft. Credit bureaus and creditors will have to comply with a number of medical privacy restrictions that ban the sharing of medical information. Title

IV of the Fair and Accurate Credit Transaction Act limits the use and sharing of medical information in the financial system and provides an updated and more expansive definition of medical information.

Under a new FACTA provision, consumer reporting agencies may not report the name, address, and telephone number of any medical creditor unless the information is provided in codes that do not identify or infer the provider of care or the individual's medical condition. Another section says a creditor may not obtain or use medical information to make credit decisions. Your consent is needed to disclose medical information to an employer or creditor. The consent request must use clear and conspicuous language about how the information will be used.

Now, what does all of this mean? It will be easier for you to dispute information on your credit report related to medical bills because the financial institutions are no longer suppose to share medical billing information with one another.

AVOID CREDIT REPAIR COMPANIES

Let me explain why credit repair companies are bad and only after a profit. Most of these companies are acting as a third party, and often they do not gain your consent, so that they can inquire and receive your credit report from the three major credit bureaus. When they are successful in gaining data, they only dispute negative items on your credit report. A major reason why it is difficult for credit repair companies to act on your behalf is because the credit bureaus hate them.

One other reason you want to stay away from credit repair companies is because they want you to pay before any services are provided. Many of them do not know all of the computer procedures when it comes to dealing with the credit bureaus so the bureaus set up obstacles for people working with credit repair companies.

RETURN SERVICE REQUESTED

FEBRUARY 03, 2004   FILE NUMBER

Thank you for contacting ▓▓▓▓▓▓▓. Our goal is to maintain
complete and accurate information on your credit report. We
have provided the information below in response to your request.

Re: Protective Statement

The protective statement on your credit report will inform all
credit grantors to contact you first before extending any credit.

To add a protective statement to your credit report, please
complete the enclosed form and return it to ▓▓▓▓▓▓▓ at the
address below, or fax it to ▓▓▓▓▓▓▓ . Upon receipt of this
completed form, we will process your request and mail you an
updated copy of your credit report.

Re: General Policy

The federal Fair Credit Reporting Act requires ▓▓▓▓▓▓▓ to
investigate, free of charge, information on your credit report
that you believe is inaccurate.

If you have reason to believe that the fee charged by a credit
repair company was too high, and/or its services were
misrepresented, please let us know if you would like your
situation to be referred for investigation by filling out and
sending us the form below. With your permission, we will provide
the information you send to the appropriate authorities. It
would also be helpful for you to attach any brochures or
documents you received from the credit repair company.

If you have any additional questions or concerns, please contact
▓▓▓▓▓▓▓ at the address shown below, or visit us on the web at
▓▓▓▓▓▓▓ for general information. When contacting our
office, please provide your current file number

FILE NUMBER

Name of Credit Repair Company _____

Contact Person's Name _____

Contact Person's Telephone # _____

Address of Credit Repair Company _____

Amount you were charged _____

What you were promised _____

Complaint _____

_____

DEBT CONSOLIDATION COMPANIES

Debt consolidation companies are not for the purpose of repairing your credit. In fact, they only serve as a bad mark. When creditors review your credit report and see you have acquired the services of a debt consolidation company, they view this as you being irresponsible and someone who cannot manage his own financial resources. Their thinking is why should they extend credit to you if you can't manage the financial responsibilities to which you are already obligated.

Debt consolidations do nothing more than extend your financial problems. If most people took the time to do their research on these companies, they would discover the truth behind them. Debt consolidation companies are nothing more than collection agencies for the banks and credit card companies to trick consumers and collect unpaid debts.

The one thing that should be a dead give away for most people is that debt consolidation companies will give you a lower payment but without a contract. This is one of the ways credit card companies can keep you in breach of the original contract.

Debt consolidation cannot hide a person from delinquent bills, judgments, or lawsuits although these companies will tell you different. They will also tell you that with their help, your credit will get better. This simply is not true. For the most part when a person gives a debt consolidation company his money, it will be deposited into interest- bearing accounts. The company will keep the first $500 to $4,000 of your payments if you stay consistent with them. Most of the time when a debt consolidation company advertises as not-for-profit, it is because it has other commercial companies that pay the bills. They are also paid through hidden fees charged to you after they have persuaded you to agree to their terms.

One of the most important things that can severely harm

a person when dealing with a debt consolidation company is power of attorney. Most people do not realize that when they enter into an agreement with one of these companies, they are giving the company power of attorney. This means the credit card company will only deal with the debt consolidation company, not you. The credit card company could lower your payments to $50 a month, but the debt consolidation company might tell you the payments were lowered to $75 a month. If you contact a credit card company regarding your account, it is no longer obligated to release information to you.

Debt consolidation companies lead people to believe that they are negotiating smaller payments. All they are doing is getting the collection rate on your monthly payments lowered, but not the actual interest rate. This happens because your collection rate is lowered. Remember, when dealing with any company that says it can help you improve your credit, it is in the business to make money. If you are already in debt and are at your financial cliff, these companies are only going to push you over the edge.

Stay away from law firms that act as credit repair companies. They are not attempting to work on your credit. The law firm's and lawyer's idea of debt consolidation or debt relief is to advise you to file bankruptcy. If they are successful in persuading you to do this, they will charge you a fee. If you do not believe me, try and find a law firm then pay them to repair your credit and see if anything gets done.

Understand that America is built off credit. What that means is that your name is everything, and when people extend you credit, you are basically acting off your name and your word. When it appears you don't value either, people or creditors become more reluctant to extend you credit.

The thing to remember when dealing with any company or individual who says they will help you consolidate or repair your credit is that they are not trying to retain you as a long-term client, therefore, they do not care about losing your business after they have gotten your money.

STAY AWAY FROM DISCLOSURE FORMS

One of the most important things to remember about the credit bureaus is that they make money by selling information about you to other companies. I have included a consumer disclosure form and credit reinvestigation forms that are used by the credit bureaus to collect more information about you, even when you think they are looking out for your best interest.

You do not want to give the credit bureaus any information they can use against you or use to make more money off your name. That is why I stress do not give them information such as your driver's license number, banking information, your spouse's name, or your parents' names. The key to beating the credit bureaus is outsmarting them at their own game of collecting information on you and storing it in their databases.

FILE NUMBER

Disclosure Request   File Number: Date:

To receive a copy of your credit report please complete this
form, attach proof of the required information, and include
payment (if necessary) before returning it to ████████ ███████
███████. If you wish, you may also use this form to purchase a
credit score and have it sent with your credit report.

Name: _____ Sr., Jr., III, IV, V, Other: _____
                          (circle one if appropriate)

Other Name(s) Used: _____ SSN: _____

Current Address: _____ Date of Birth: _____

                 _____ Home Phone: _____

Previous Address: _____ Driver's
                                  License #: _____

                 _____

____I request the following statement to be added to my file
(please check if appropriate):

        Fraud Victim Alert: Fraudulent Applications may be submitted
        in my name using correct personal information. Do not extend
        credit without first contacting me personally and verifying
        all applicant information at:

        Home Phone: _____ Work Phone: _____

        Signature: _____

Include Payment (if necessary):
If you have experienced a denial of credit based on your
████████ credit report within the past 60 days, you are
entitled to a free copy of your report. Otherwise, you may be
required to purchase the report. The fee for this, based on the
state you live in, is listed below. If you would like to receive
your ████████ Consumer Credit Score in addition to the credit
report, please provide additional payment.

        ████████ Credit Report - $ 9.00
        ████████ Credit Score - $ 4.95

        __ Check here to include credit score with credit report

CC Type: ( )Amer. Express ( )Visa ( )MasterCard ( )Discover

Credit Card Number: _____ Exp. Date: _____

Customer Signature: _____

Request for Investigation   File Number:

Should you wish to initiate an investigation, you may do by completing and returning this form to the address listed below.

Upon receipt of your request, an investigation will be initiated and completed within 30 days. Upon completion, you will receive written notice of the results of your investigation. We recommend that you do not apply for credit while your request for an investigation is pending.

1   If any of this information in the box on the left is incorrect or incomplete, write the corrections in the boxes on the right.

Name:	Name:
Other Name(s):	Other Name(s):
Address:	Address:
Date of Birth:	Date of Birth:
Driver's License Number:	Driver's License Number:
Telephone Number(s):	Telephone Number(s):
Employer:	Employer:

2   Tell us what you disagree with on your credit report. Use the additional space on the back of this form if necessary.

Company Name:	Company Name:
Account #:	Account #:

The reason I disagree:
- ☐ This is not my account
- ☐ I have never paid late
- ☐ This account is in bankruptcy
- ☐ This account is closed
- ☐ I have paid this account in full
- ☐ I paid this before it went to collection or before it was charged off
- ☐ Other:

The reason I disagree:
- ☐ This is not my account
- ☐ I have never paid late
- ☐ This account is in bankruptcy
- ☐ This account is closed
- ☐ I have paid this account in full
- ☐ I paid this before it went to collection or before it was charged off
- ☐ Other:

Signature:

Return this form to:

RESEARCH REQUEST FORM

Upon completion, please return this document to the following address:

Or, if you prefer, you may initiate an investigation request via the Internet at:

Confirmation Number:

Intentionally making any false statement to a consumer reporting agency for the purpose of having it placed on a consumer report is punishable by law in some states.

If your identifying information differs from the information listed on this form, please fill in the correct information in the space provided below each item.

Please provide a photocopy of your driver's license, social security card, or a recent utility bill that reflects the correct information.

Name: SS #:   DOB:

Current Address:

Previous Address(es):

Employment:

Daytime Phone Number: Evening Phone Number:

List other names which you have used for credit in the past.

Collection Agency Information

Collection Agency Name _____ Account Number _____
Reason for investigation: ☐ Not Mine   ☐ Collection Paid in Full   ☐ Paid Before Collection Status

☐ Other (Please explain) _____

Collection Agency Name _____ Account Number _____
Reason for investigation: ☐ Not Mine   ☐ Collection Paid in Full   ☐ Paid Before Collection Status

☐ Other (Please explain) _____

Credit Account Information

Company Name _____ Account Number _____
Reason for investigation: ☐ Not Mine   ☐ Paid in Full   ☐ Current/Previous Payment Status Incorrect   ☐ Account Closed

☐ Other (Please explain) _____

Company Name _____ Account Number _____
Reason for investigation: ☐ Not Mine   ☐ Paid in Full   ☐ Current/Previous Payment Status Incorrect   ☐ Account Closed

☐ Other (Please explain) _____

Company Name _____ Account Number _____
Reason for investigation: ☐ Not Mine   ☐ Paid in Full   ☐ Current/Previous Payment Status Incorrect   ☐ Account Closed

☐ Other (Please explain) _____

Company Name _____ Account Number _____
Reason for investigation: ☐ Not Mine   ☐ Paid in Full   ☐ Current/Previous Payment Status Incorrect   ☐ Account Closed

☐ Other (Please explain) _____

How Tax ID NUMBERS Work

The following method is included as information only. It may be considered illegal if used in the wrong way. If you want further explanation, you should consult an attorney.

Tax ID numbers (TIN) or Employer ID Numbers (EIN) are used for the purpose of business identification by the government and the IRS, as well as for paying taxes.

To put it plain and simple, they are old Social Security numbers of deceased people that are regenerated by the IRS. When companies apply for an EIN they are really receiving an old Social Security number.

Listed below are the beginning Social Security numbers. The Social Security administration assigns by state to immigrants and newborn babies who are virtually unknown in the beginning.

001-003 NH	400-407 KY	530 NV
004-007 ME	408-415 TN	531-539 WA
008-009 VT	416-424 AL	540-544 OR
010-034 MA	425-428 MS	545-573 CA
035-039 RI	429-432 AR	574 AK
040-049 CT	433-439 LA	575-576 HI
050-134 NY	440-448 OK	577-579 DC
135-158 NJ	449-467 TX	580 VI Virgin Islands
159-211 PA	468-477 MN	581-584 PR Puerto Rico
212-220 MD	478-485 IA	585 NM
221-222 DE	486-500 MO	586 PI Pacific Islands*
223-231 VA	501-502 ND	587-588 MS
232-236 WV	503-504 SD	589-595 FL
237-246 NC	505-508 NE	596-599 PR Puerto Rico
247-251 SC	509-515 KS	600-601 AZ
252-260 GA	516-517 MT	602-626 CA
261-267 FL	518-519 ID	627-645 TX
268-302 OH	520 WY	646-647 UT

303-317 IN	521-524 CO	648-649 NM
318-361 IL	525 NM	*Guam, American Samoa,
362-386 MI	526-527 AZ	Philippine Islands,
387-399 WI	528-529 UT	Northern Mariana Islands

650-699 unassigned, for future use
700-728 Railroad workers through 1963, then discontinued
729-799 unassigned, for future use
800-999 not valid Social Security numbers.

Some sources have claimed that numbers above 900 were used when some state programs were converted to federal control, but current Social Security Administration documents claim no numbers above 799 have ever been used.

HOW TO OBTAIN A TAX ID NUMBER

To obtain a tax ID number you must complete a form like the one on the following page or you can simply call the IRS at 800-829-1040 and receive it.

Form **SS-4**	**Application for Employer Identification Number**	EIN	
(Rev. April 2000) Department of the Treasury Internal Revenue Service	(For use by employers, corporations, partnerships, trusts, estates, churches, government agencies, certain individuals, and others. See instructions.) ▶ **Keep a copy for your records.**		OMB No. 1545-0003

Please type or print clearly.

1   Name of applicant (legal name) (see instructions)

2 Trade name of business (if different from name on line 1)	**3** Executor, trustee, "care of" name

4a Mailing address (street address) (room, apt., or suite no.)	**5a** Business address (if different from address on lines 4a and 4b)

4b City, state, and ZIP code	**5b** City, state, and ZIP code

6   County and state where principal business is located

7   Name of principal officer, general partner, grantor, owner, or trustor—SSN or ITIN may be required (see instructions) ▶

8a   Type of entity (Check only one box.) (see instructions)

    Caution: *If applicant is a limited liability company, see the instructions for line 8a.*

☐ Sole proprietor (SSN) _____   ☐ Estate (SSN of decedent) _____
☐ Partnership   ☐ Personal service corp.   ☐ Plan administrator (SSN) _____
☐ REMIC   ☐ National Guard   ☐ Other corporation (specify) ▶ _____
☐ State/local government   ☐ Farmers' cooperative   ☐ Trust
☐ Church or church-controlled organization   ☐ Federal government/military
☐ Other nonprofit organization (specify) ▶ _____   (enter GEN if applicable) _____
☐ Other (specify) ▶

8b   If a corporation, name the state or foreign country (if applicable) where incorporated

State	Foreign country

9   Reason for applying (Check only one box.) (see instructions)
☐ Started new business (specify type) ▶ _____
☐ Banking purpose (specify purpose) ▶ _____
☐ Changed type of organization (specify new type) ▶ _____
☐ Hired employees (Check the box and see line 12.)   ☐ Purchased going business
☐ Created a pension plan (specify type) ▶   ☐ Created a trust (specify type) ▶ _____
☐ Other (specify) ▶

10   Date business started or acquired (month, day, year) (see instructions) | **11** Closing month of accounting year (see instructions)

12   First date wages or annuities were paid or will be paid (month, day, year). **Note:** *If applicant is a withholding agent, enter date income will first be paid to nonresident alien.* (month, day, year) . . . . ▶

13   Highest number of employees expected in the next 12 months. **Note:** *If the applicant does not expect to have any employees during the period, enter -0-.* (see instructions) . . . . ▶

Nonagricultural	Agricultural	Household

14   Principal activity (see instructions) ▶

15   Is the principal business activity manufacturing? . . . . ☐ Yes   ☐ No
    If "Yes," principal product and raw material used ▶

16   To whom are most of the products or services sold? Please check one box.   ☐ Business (wholesale)
    ☐ Public (retail)   ☐ Other (specify) ▶   ☐ N/A

17a   Has the applicant ever applied for an employer identification number for this or any other business? . . . . ☐ Yes   ☐ No
    Note: *If "Yes," please complete lines 17b and 17c.*

17b   If you checked "Yes" on line 17a, give applicant's legal name and trade name shown on prior application, if different from line 1 or 2 above.
    Legal name ▶   Trade name ▶

17c   Approximate date when and city and state where the application was filed. Enter previous employer identification number if known.

Approximate date when filed (mo., day, year)	City and state where filed	Previous EIN

Under penalties of perjury, I declare that I have examined this application, and to the best of my knowledge and belief, it is true, correct, and complete.

	Business telephone number (include area code) ( )
	Fax telephone number (include area code) ( )

Name and title (Please type or print clearly.) ▶

Signature ▶   Date ▶

Note: *Do not write below this line. For official use only.*

Please leave blank ▶	Geo.	Ind.	Class	Size	Reason for applying

For Privacy Act and Paperwork Reduction Act Notice, see page 4.   Cat. No. 16055N   Form **SS-4** (Rev. 4-2000)

The technique of using the EIN to repair your credit is finding out if you have a good number that will not be flagged by the credit bureaus. The first step would be to make sure you have the proper identification. What I mean by this is that you must make sure that your Social Security number is not listed on your driver's license. People are using tax ID numbers to replace their Social Security number on loan applications.

Using the next steps will keep credit obtained under your Social Security number separate from credit obtained under your tax ID number. Remember you will be lying on your credit application if you use this number in place of your Social Security number.

This is illegal on certain applications dealing with anything such as, FHA, VA, or HUD loans. You will be violating federal law, and if convicted you could receive a $250,000 fine and five years in federal prison.

There are some states that are prosecuting at state level for giving false information on your loan application. If you fill out an application and write "EIN" next to where it says Social Security number I do not see how you would be lying on your application because you are telling the company it is not a Social Security number. If you use this new account to purchase things on credit with the intention of not repaying the loan, you are committing fraud.

When using an EIN/TIN to repair your credit, you should open up a checking and savings account at a local bank, preferably a credit union. There are very critical things you must understand about how the credit bureaus' computer systems are set up to establish new credit files.

Remember, the computer systems at the credit bureaus operate off a matching technique using your last name, your first name, your date of birth, with your street mailing address, and your five digit zip code. The computer system can easily be thrown off if you use a new zip code or if you change your birth date by two or three days.

Let's say your name is John Doe, your real date of birth is May 14, 1964, and your mailing zip code is 34678. To throw off the computer system, you could simply change your birth date by a few days and use the zip code of a family member or friend. The best way to get started with establishing credit with an EIN would be to apply for a secured credit card since you know you won't be turned down.

Once you have established the credit account and maintained it for maybe six months, you may then apply for unsecured credit accounts, such as a gas card or a department store account. If at any point you make a mistake and use information from your true credit file such as your actual date of birth, the computer systems at the credit bureaus will automatically merge your new credit file with your old one.

As an alternative, you can also apply for a Dun and Bradstreet account, which can be obtained by calling 800-234-3867. Dun and Bradstreet was established for the purpose of maintaining business credit reports, and once you receive a number, you can use it to apply for credit in your business name using a DUNS number on all applications.

CREATING A NEW CREDIT FILE LEGALLY

There are many ways of trying to outsmart the credit bureaus illegally, but this method is completely legal, if you follow the instructions carefully.

You can establish a new credit file by simply legally changing your name. Go to your local courthouse with a notarized name change petition for a new name and name change order. You can change your last name, your first and last name, your middle and last name, or your complete full name. Your new last name should not start with the first letter of your current last name. After you have followed these steps consider yourself a new person with a new identity. The next thing you must do is change your address. You may use one of your friend's or relative's addresses that is different from yours or rent a PO Box. Remember, it cannot be an address you have used before.

When you have established a new address, you should take your new name change order to the Social Security office and ask for a new card. You will receive your same number but it will be under your new name. This will not affect anything legally or your benefits. By getting a new card with your new name, you have just created another new computer record under federal law. Now that you have your new card, take your new name change order to the DMV to update and change your state driver's license. You will receive a new number under your new name and new address. This changes your identity and creates a new computer DMV record. If you are stopped for speeding, only your name and new address are retained. Your previous DMV record will not show up unless you are arrested. This is very important because remember that Experian owns AutoCheck, which contains vehicle registration for any car you have purchased that contains your old driver's license record. In addition to that, Equifax owns ChoicePoint. Getting your new driver's license under your new name enables you to receive lower car insurance rates, even if you have previous accidents or speeding tickets.

Once you get your new driver's license, change your name on your auto title and registration. You can get auto insurance cheaper with no negatives on your registration. When you change your driver's license and the name and address on your automobile registration, title, and auto insurance, you have instantly created a legally clean driving record, a new DMV record, and a new auto insurance file under your new name. Now, there won't be any points against you for speeding tickets, accidents, and moving violations. Remember that when you apply for insurance not only do the insurance companies run a credit check at some agencies, they also use a system called car sweep.

If you have a job, inform your employer of your new name and have them change you employment records to reflect it. This gives you a good job record for your new identity, especially if you have been there for a long period of time. The next step is to send a certified copy of your new name change order to the Health department or vital statistics in the state where you were born and ask them to send you a certified new birth certificate reflecting your new name. You will need this for passports. You should also send a certified copy of your new name change order to all schools you've attended and request they change your name and that they send you a certified copy of your school records and diplomas or degrees earned.

Finally, apply for a credit card over the Internet or locally, which establishes your new file with all three credit bureaus instantly. Your new credit file will be blank and will have no credit on it, so do not be tempted to contact a company with whom you have good credit and have the company put this good account under your new name. Do not report any credit you had before your name change. If you do, the credit bureaus will enter not just the good credit, but all the bad stuff under both your old and new name since the files will be cross-referenced. This mistake will make your new credit file merge with your old one, then you will have bad credit again, and all the work you have done will be useless. The only other way to establish a new credit file other than being an authorized user under another person's credit is opening a savings account and applying for a secured credit card at your local bank. Remember to do this after you apply for a credit card over the Internet or locally establish your new credit file with each of the credit bureaus. The last thing to remember about this process is that if the police run your new name, this initial entry will establish a new police record and FBI file as long as you are not fingerprinted. If you break the law and are arrested, your fingerprints will show your old and new identities. This is important because most employers do background and credit checks, and when your old and new names are cross-referenced, the employer will know you were once not creditworthy as far as corporate America is concerned.

OPENING CHECKING ACCOUNT EVEN WHEN BANKS WON'T LET YOU

There is a vast majority of the population in the United States who cannot open a checking account because they have (1) bad credit, (2) an outstanding check with Telecheck or Chexsystems, or (3) have been a victim of identity theft. If you have this problem, don't worry. There is a way for you to open a checking account.

There are two types of checking and savings account. One is for personal and the other is for commercial, otherwise known as a business checking account. The only thing that you need to open a business checking account is a business license, tax ID number, and articles of incorporation from the state in which you have obtained your business license. All this may seem complicated to some, but it is very simple.

Your first step in opening a business checking account is to obtain a tax ID number. As I've mentioned, this can be done by calling the IRS at 800-829-1040 or filling out an SS4 application. Now, keep in mind that when you call, you must have a business name in mind. You can use your home address as the business location. When you call the IRS, you must follow the prompts and request the business tax option. Once you have a live operator on the phone, he will assist you in obtaining your tax ID or employer identification number.

Once you have your tax ID number, the next thing you should do is file for your articles of incorporation within the state you live. This should not cost more than a hundred dollars. In order to get the necessary papers to incorporate, you should contact the Secretary of State's office located in your state capitol. The reason you should have your business incorporated is because sometimes banks will want you to open a regular account if you are a sole proprietor.

After you have received your articles of incorporation, purchase your business license. The fee for obtaining it will be no more than fifty dollars. Once you have your license, tax ID number, and articles of incorporation, you are now ready to open a business checking account.

Keep in mind that some banks will run your Social Security number through Chexsystems even when you are opening a business account. There are some banks, such as Bank of America that will not. Bank of America simply checks to make sure your tax ID number is valid. For those banks that still use your Social Security number along with your tax ID number, there is a way to get around that as well. If you run into this problem, you should find someone close whom you trust and who is not listed with Chexsystems and use them as the authorized signer on the account. This will prevent the bank from having to run your name through Chexsystems.

After the account has been open, you should have the business check card and pin number forwarded to your home address (business address). To prevent the individual who is the authorized signer from getting any money out of the account without your knowledge. The last thing to remember is there is no need to order checks because you will have a debt card with PIN number in hand.

IDENTITY THEFT

One of the fastest growing crimes in America is identity theft. Having someone steal your identity can turn your life upside down if you do not understand how to fight it and the laws that govern the creditors and the credit bureaus.

Have you ever had something on your credit that did not belong to you and when you contacted the credit bureaus, they told you to contact the creditor, only for the creditor to say contact the credit bureaus? Well, this is no longer a problem if you know your rights.

When you have something on your credit that may be fraudulent or you suspect it to be fraud, simply go to your local police station and file a police report for the items. If the police department does not want to take a police report from you, do not let this discourage you. The Federal Trade Commission has provided the following information when it comes to filing a police report: "Local authorities may tell you that they can't take a report. Stress the importance of a police report. Many creditors require one to resolve your dispute. Also remind them that under their voluntary Police Report Initiative, credit bureaus will automatically block the fraudulent accounts and bad debts from appearing on your credit report, but only if you can give them a copy of the police report. If you can't get the local police to take a report, try your county police. If that doesn't work, try your state police. If you are told that identity theft is not a crime under your state law, ask to file a Miscellaneous Incident Report instead."

Once you have done this, send a copy of your police report to the three major credit bureaus. They will automatically remove these items from your credit file. This may take up to thirty days. The great part about this is that the stress and the burden of proof fall back on the creditor. You are probably thinking that this is simply not that easy, but it is indeed.

There is a little law called the Fair and Accurate Credit Transactions Act, which was passed in December 2003. This law basically outlines the following guidelines:

1. It requires the presence of a fraud alert on a consumer's credit report and requires additional verification before issuing credit;

2. It gives consumers the right to obtain financial records from businesses where thieves used their names;

3. It gives consumers the right to block fraudulent trade lines otherwise known as credit account information from appearing on their credit reports;

4. It gives consumers the right to make one call to the bureaus to obtain fraud alerts on all three reports;

5. It imposes new account opening verification standards and rules against "repollution" on reports with previously deleted fraudulent accounts.

Some rights may require consumers to provide businesses or credit bureaus with a notarized ID theft affidavit or a copy of the filed police report. Trust me when I tell you the creditor will never attempt to dispute your fraudulent claim. Remember that all three credit bureaus operate off a computer system (E-

OSCAR) that updates every thirty or sixty days, but every thirty days more than likely. Consider sending your disputes to more than one department at the various credit bureaus. To place a fraud alert on your credit file call the following:

Experian—888-397-3742
Equifax—888-766-0008
TransUnion—800-680-7289

FILE FREEZE

A file freeze is very important to you as a consumer because it gives you the ability to control your own credit file. This bill was passed in 2003, and it allows consumers to place a security freeze on their file. This stops credit bureaus from releasing information to credit grantors without the consumer's express authorization or by law. The file freeze bill has only been passed in nine states: Connecticut, Massachusetts, Nevada, New Mexico, New Jersey, New York, Texas, Vermont, and California. This is another weapon you, the consumer, can use against the credit bureaus. They do not like it, simply because they see it as a hassle, and it gives them less control over your credit file. The freeze will block access to your credit period. That means nothing can happen unless you personally release the freeze by contacting the credit bureaus and giving them your PIN code. Things such as information that does not belong to you and may have been placed on your credit due to fraud can be taken off. If you do not live in one of the states that has already passed this bill giving consumers the right to place a file freeze on their credit, don't worry. This bill will eventually affect every state in the country since identity theft is the fastest growing crime in America.

I hope you have discovered something in this book you will find useful in your efforts to restore your credit and your good name. Remember that only those who are not afraid to take risks may truly discover the wealth of the world. Financial power is held by those with the best information and the most fearless attitude to expand their wealth. I challenge anyone who has read this book to stop giving in to the herd instinct. That means challenge those things that everyone else assumes to be correct. People need to fight their fears and develop a sense of faith. Lord Mansfield's ancient concept was "no man shall enrich himself unjustly at the expense of another." This is exactly what the rich are doing to the poor. There is a price to be paid for knowledge, but there is also a reward for those willing to pay that price. The only way to overcome the problem of credit or the pressure of education is wealth. One thing that the Japanese and Chinese would do in order to create a similar or better product than the American brand is buy an American product, take it apart to examine how it was assembled, then they would build a better product. This is what we all should practice.

Examine politics, economics, credit bureaus, religion, and education. The only way to put a puzzle together is to take it apart. Thomas Jefferson once said, "If a nation expects to be ignorant and free, it expects something that cannot be." I relate that to individuals who just follow or assume without question. Financial freedom will never come where ignorance exists. This book was not written to create some type of radical or illegal actions. It was written simply with the message to wake up and discover your wealth because it does not always come by way of education or employment from someone else.

DISPUTE LETTERS

This section of the book has been completely dedicated to dispute letters that you may use for the purpose of disputing anything on your credit report. These letters range from inquiries to questioning inaccurate or fraudulent credit card accounts. Please keep in mind that anytime you use one of these letters, send it certified by mail. This is a good way of recordkeeping. Also, remember that you should try and keep a file of every credit report that you receive from the credit bureaus. For example you should file all information pertaining to TransUnion, Equifax and Experian together.

Sample Letter 1—Removal of Information that Does Not Belong on your credit

Date
Name
Address
City, State, Zip

Credit Bureau
Address
City, State, Zip

To Whom It May Concern:

I am writing this letter in an effort to remove inaccurate information from my credit report. The following information you have placed on my file has seriously affected my credit profile. Please be reminded that it is important that credit bureaus maintain accurate information per the Fair Credit Reporting Act.

The following account does not belong to me and should be removed from my credit report immediately:
(List account and account numbers).

Sincerely,
Your Signature
Your Name

Sample Letter 2—Removal of Outdated Information from Your Credit Report

Date
Name
Address
City, State, Zip

Credit Bureau
Address
City, State, Zip

To Whom It May Concern:

After looking at my credit report, I noticed several outdated and inaccurate items:
(List account, account number and brief explanation of why it's inaccurate).
Please investigate these inaccurate items and remove them immediately.

Sincerely,
Your Signature
Your Name

Sample Letter 3—Follow-up Letter When You Do Not Get a Response the First Time

Date
Name
Address
City, State, Zip

Credit Bureau
Address
City, State, Zip
RE: Account Number

To Whom It May Concern:

This is a certified letter being sent in response to my first letter concerning the above account. Please be advised that by law your company is required to respond to my request within thirty days. Your company has failed to follow such guidelines and is in violation of the Fair Credit Reporting Act and may be reported and investigated under these circumstances. Please be aware that I am keeping records of each date that I have contacted your company by registered mail and am prepared to use this information in case I must take you to court concerning this matter.

Sincerely,
Your Signature
Your Name

Sample Letter 4—Letter to Stop Collection Agency from Obtaining a Debt from You

Date
Name
Address
City, State, Zip

Collection Agency
Address
City, State, Zip
Account Name/Number

To Whom It May Concern:

I am requesting that your company discontinue its efforts to collect on the above account. By law I do not have to deal with your agency as it relates to this account, therefore, you should stop contacting me. I have made arrangements with the original creditor to settle this matter.

Sincerely,
Your Signature
Your Name

Sample Letter 5—Letter to Bureaus after Collection Agency Can't Prove You Owe

Date
Name
Address
City, State, Zip

Credit Bureau
Address
City, State, Zip
RE: Name/Number of account you are disputing

To Whom It May Concern:

This letter is being written to dispute the above account, which I have done several times. You have responded by stating that the creditor or collection agency verified the account. I have contacted the collection agency/creditor on several occasions as well, and they have yet to respond to my dispute, therefore, your company could not have reached them concerning this debt.The Fair Credit Reporting Act requires that you respond to my dispute within thirty days as well as verify its accuracy. If the account cannot be verified, your company must delete the account from my credit report. If you cannot show proof that you have verified this debt and you continue to list this item on my credit report, I am prepared to sue your company under the Fair Credit Reporting Act.

Sincerely,
Your Signature
Your Name

Sample Letter 6—Letter to Validate a Debt

Date
Name
Address
City, State, Zip

Collection Agency
Address
City, State, Zip
Re: Include Account Name/ Number

To Whom It May Concern:

I am writing to inform you I have been a victim of identity theft, and many accounts were established without my consent. This letter is to inform your company I am disputing this debt and have filed a police report. I have a right under the Fair Debt Collections Practices Act to request validation of the bill for which your company is requesting payment. I am asking that you send me proof this account belongs to me as well as any agreement obligating me to it. Please be informed that reporting inaccurate information to the credit bureaus is a defamation of character. I am requesting that this letter be forwarded to your legal department since non-compliance with it may be in violation with the Federal Trade Commission and other federal agencies.

Sincerely,
Your Signature
Your Name

Sample Letter 7—Remove Inquiries from Credit Report
Date
Name
Address
City, State, Zip

Credit Bureau
Address
City, State, Zip
Re: Unauthorized Credit Inquiry *(Include Account Number)*

To Whom It May Concern:

I recently received a copy of my credit report, and I noticed an inquiry that I did not authorize and of which I do not have knowledge. Please be advised that by law no inquiry can be placed on my credit without my authorization. I am requesting that this inquiry be removed immediately from my credit report.

Please send me an updated copy of my credit report after this inaccurate information has been removed.

Sincerely,
Your Signature
Your Name

Sample Letter 8—To Remove Inquiries

Date
Name
Address
City, State, Zip

Credit Bureau
Address
City, State, Zip
Re: Fraudulent Credit Inquiry

To Whom It May Concern:

Recently, I received a copy of my credit report which showed inquiries that I did not authorize. I understand you should not be allowed to put an inquiry on my file unless I have approved it. I have provided you with a police report, and I am currently working with an investigator to stop the use of my name by someone who has stolen my identity. Please have the following inquiries removed from my credit file immediately because I did not authorize them and they are fraudulent.

(List Fraudulent Inquiries):

Also be advised the Fair Credit Reporting Act states that any information that is maintained on an individual's credit report must be accurate. This includes unauthorized inquiries.

If your company refuses to investigate and respond to my request within 30 days from the receipt of this certified letter, I am prepared to file a lawsuit in small claims court. Also, be aware that the return receipt/signature of this certified letter is evidence of your receipt of said request.

I have sent this letter because I need your prompt response to this issue, and I need written correspondence as evidence your company is acting upon my request. If you find that I am remiss and you do have my authorization to inquire into my credit report, and then please send me proof likewise.

Sincerely,
Your Signature
Your Name

Sample letter 9—Letter to Remove Fraudulent Accounts

Date

Name

Address

City, State, Zip

Credit Bureau

Address

City, State, Zip

To Whom It May Concern:

Please accept this letter as a written request to dispute the following account information of items appearing on my credit report. To prevent any confusion, I have listed the item and account number below:

(List account, account number and explanation)

I am requesting that the following account be removed immediately from my credit report. I am seeking further legal advice in addition to working with a police investigator to locate the individual(s) who is responsible for fraudulently establishing this account without my permission or authorization. I have tried to work with your credit reporting agency as well as the credit grantor to have this account removed from my credit report. If I am unsuccessful with this attempt, I will be forced to file a suit in federal court naming your credit reporting agency, the above creditor, collection agencies, and the acceptor of this letter as defendants.

It is my understanding that per, the Fair Credit Reporting Act, this request must be given attention and completed within 30 days of your receipt. Thank you for your prompt attention to this matter.

Sincerely,

Your Name

Your Signature

Sample Letter 10—Letter to place file freeze on credit
If you would like to place a file freeze on your credit report, you can use the following letter:

Date
Credit Bureau Name
Address
City, State, Zip

To Whom It May Concern:

I am requesting that a security freeze be placed on my credit file. My personal information below will assist you in locating my file:
Name
Address
Social Security Number
File Number (if you have one)

I have also enclosed a copy of a police report as proof that I have been a victim of fraud. Please act promptly on my request.

Sincerely,
Your Signature
Your Name

Sample Letter 11—Dispute Letter

Date
Name
Address
City, State, Zip

Credit Bureau Name
Address
City, State, Zip

To Whom It May Concern:

I request that the following inaccurate items be immediately investigated. They must be removed in order to show my true credit history, as these items should not be on my report. Pursuant to the Fair Credit Reporting Act I will expect you to complete the verification within thirty days.

(Company name and account number)

Please send me my updated report as soon as your investigation is completed.

Sincerely,
Your Signature
Your Name

Sample Letter 12—Remaining Items
Date
Name
Address
City, State, Zip

Credit Bureau Name
Address
City, State, Zip
RE: Name/Account Number

To Whom It May Concern:

Thank you for deleting some of the accounts that incorrectly appeared on my credit report. However, I still dispute the remaining items. These accounts are still being reported inaccurately and are extremely damaging to my credit:

In accordance with the Fair Credit Reporting Act section 168i, your company is required to reinvestigate these items and delete them. Please send me an updated copy of my report as soon as the investigation is complete.

I would appreciate the name of the individuals you contacted for verification along with their address and phone number so I may follow up.

Sincerely,
Your Signature
Your Name

Sample Letter 13—Response Letter to Credit Bureau Verification Process

Date
Name
Address
City, State, Zip

Credit Bureau
Address
City, State, Zip

To Whom It May Concern:

In accordance with the law, I have sent the attached letter to creditors in order to confirm the debts you say I owe. Since these creditors cannot verify these debts, even though I am the alleged debtor, your bureau could not have verified these items.

I demand that you remove all reference to those accounts from my credit report within thirty days.

Sincerely,
Your Signature
Your Name

Sample Letter 14—Follow up letter when bureau did not respond to dispute letter

Date
Name
Address
City, State, Zip

Credit Bureau
Address
City, State, Zip

To Whom It May Concern:

I am enclosing a copy of a letter that I mailed to you requesting that you verify the alleged debt your company claims I owe. The return receipt, a copy of which I enclosed, was signed on (date). More than thirty days have passed, and I have not yet received proof that you have validated the debt.

Therefore, in accordance with s.1629e(8)of the Debt Collection Practices Act, which clearly states that any information known to be false, cannot be reported to any credit bureau, I request that you immediately delete this information from my credit report.

Please send me a copy of my updated credit report as soon as the above has been completed.

Sincerely,
Your Signature
Your Name

Sample Letter 15—Response to Credit Repair Service

Date
Name
Address
City, State, Zip

Credit Bureau
Address
City, State, Zip

To Whom It May Concern:

In response to you letter stating that I am using a credit repair service, you are mistaken.

The Fair Credit Reporting Act obligates you to investigate any disputed claim within thirty days. So far, you have not fulfilled your obligation to do so and are in clear violation of the law.

I am not using nor have I ever used a credit repair service. I am prepared to take advantage of the protection of the law.

I expect you to begin and complete the verification process within thirty days from your receipt of this letter. If I do not receive confirmation of this within that time, I will forward a copy of all correspondence together with a formal complaint to the Federal Trade Commission and the subcommittee on banking and finance.

Sincerely,
Your Signature
Your Name

Sample Letter 16—Challenge to Verification Process to Collection Agency

Date

Name

Address

City, State, Zip

Collection Agency

Address

City, State, Zip

To Whom It May Concern:

I have received a letter claiming that I owe a debt to (name). Since this is in erroor, I request that you send me the following proof as you are obligated to do in accordance with the Debt Collection Practices Act, section 1692g.

A. The original application or contract.

B. Any and all statements allegedly related to this debt.

C. Any and all signed receipts.

D. Any and all cancelled checks.

Under the law, you have thirty days to supply this proof. In addition, do not contact me again via phone. From now on, we will communicate through mail.

Sincerely,

Your Signature

Your Name

Sample Letter 17—Request to Remove Bankruptcy Information

Date
Name
Address
City, State, Zip

Credit Bureau
Address
City, State, Zip

To Whom It May Concern:

I am disturbed that you continue to list a dismissed (filed) bankruptcy as confirmed. I am aware that you receive your information from a third party verification system known as a pacer system. This system is sometimes inaccurate because of the limitations of providing a complete Social Security number. Although it is your policy to keep reporting bankruptcy that is filed, dismissed, or adjudicated for 10 years, the Fair Credit Reporting Act mentions nothing in Section 1681c relating to bankruptcy about dismissals or filings. The law clearly states from "date of adjudication" or date of "order for relief."

Any case, civil or otherwise, which is dismissed, no longer exists in the eyes of the law, and a case filed may never have actually been adjudicated. You have no right to maintain information which the government has deemed non-existent. It is only fair that in accordance with section 1681(a)(5) of the Fair Credit Reporting Act you delete this from my credit report and send me an updated copy.

Considering it does not require an investigation, I would appreciate your response within two weeks from the date you receive this letter.

Sincerely,
Your Signature
Your Name

Sample Letter 18—Dispute of Unauthorized Credit Inquiry
Date
Name
Address
City, State, Zip

Credit Bureau
Address
City, State, Zip

RE: Unauthorized Credit Inquiry

To Whom It May Concern:

The following inquiries were not authorized by me. Please delete them. I have never given my permission for any company to inquire about my credit status. Any inquiries made are unauthorized. The presence of these inquiries on my credit report constitutes inaccurate information, which under the Fair Credit Reporting Act must be removed.
(Company Name and inquiry date)
Once your investigation is complete please send me an updated copy of my credit report. I would appreciate the name, address, and phone number of the companies who inquired about my credit so that I may follow up.

Sincerely,
Your Signature
Your Name

Sample Letter 19—Request for Removal of Outdated Information

Date
Name
Address
City, State, Zip

Credit Bureau
Address
City, State, Zip

To Whom It May Concern:

I have received my current credit report, and I need to bring to you attention several entries that are outdated.
(Account name and number)
These accounts are more than seven years old and exceed the statutory time period.Under the Fair Credit Reporting Act, they must be removed. Please send my updated/revised credit report to me after these accounts have been deleted. Your prompt attention to this matter is greatly appreciated.

Sincerely,
Your Signature
Your Name

Sample Letter 20—Request to Add Positive Information to Credit Report

Date

Name

Address

City, State, Zip

Credit Bureau

Address

City, State, Zip

To Whom It May Concern:

In reviewing my credit report, I discovered that my file fails to include information that I know is important to providing a complete portrait of me as a consumer. I request that you add the following information to my credit file:

Creditor

Address

City, State, Zip

Account Number

If you need additional information from me, I can be reached at (include phone number). Please inform me if there is a fee for this service.

Sincerely,

Your Signature

Your Name

Sample Letter 21—Proof of Contract Request

Date
Name
Address
City, State, Zip

Company Name
Address
City, State, Zip

RE: Account Number

I am in receipt of your company's letter informing me you are handling the collection of the account mentioned above. However, after reviewing my records, I am unable to find any documentation of any contractual relationship between (name of company) and me which makes you a person entitled to enforce a commercial claim against me. This letter is not a request for verification or validation.

This is a request for proof of contract to substantiate your claim. Provide me with a certified copy of an original contract, with my signature, specifically naming your company as a person entitled to enforce a commercial claim against me. Certification can be done through the presence of a notary public, who duly swears the copy made is in fact a copy of the original paper contract in question.

Failure to respond and provide strict proof of contract will constitute your tactic agreement that you, (name of president) and (name of company), are not entitled to enforce a claim against me. In the event you continue your collection efforts against me without providing proof of contract, I will file a complaint with the Attorney General and Federal Trade Commission, and file a police report against you for harassment and invasion of privacy.

You have 30 days to provide strict proof of contract. In the event you cannot provide strict proof of contract, you must cease and desist any and all collection efforts and immediately remove any derogatory information reported to the consumer reporting agencies. If you transfer this account to an attorney without providing proof of contract, he will be immediately reported to the State Bar Association and Professional Liability Fund for code of ethics violations.

Sincerely,
Your Signature
Your Name

CONTACT TELEPHONE
AND FAX NUMBERS

I have heard quite often that people have trouble getting a live voice at the three major credit bureaus. Regardless to trouble that you may have experienced in the past, all of that is about to change right now.

I have divided each credit bureau up into different sections, with the names and contacts of every possible individual with whom you will need to speak with name and department location. Each reference provided is accurate and reliable at the time of this printing I hope that these names and numbers help you as much as they helped me as I was trying to improve my credit.

Experian
    Experian: 888-397-3742
    Experian Order Line: 714-830-7000
    Marketing Department: 800-831-5614
    Fax Number: 714-830-2599
    Public Records Manager (Connie Rothacker): 714-830-7746
    Mailroom Manager (Connie Walker): 972-390-3551

Fraud Department (Shannon Stafford): 972-390-3670
National Resource Center: 800-831-5614, option 3
Direct Number to Consumer Relations: 888-567-8688, extension 5247
Top Data Customer Support (Lynn Mason): 714-830-7744
Experian (Karen Roberson): 714-830-7055
Experian (Rebecca Ferry): 714-830-7940
Experian (Rebecca Ferry) Fax: 714-830-2599
Experian (Tim Lane): 714-830-5220
Experian (Joyce Kobeshia): 714-830-7055

Equifax

Switchboard: 404-885-8000
Ordering System: 888-685-1111
Ordering System: 404-885-8300
Information Service Center: 888-295-0132
Fraud Assistance Department: 800-525-6285
Fax: 866-414-9001
Fax: 414-702-2622
Fax (Legal Department): 678-795-7954
Ordering System (Live Voice): 770-752-1158
Fax: 866-414-9005
General Services: 800-685-5000
Mortgage Department: 888-956-2970
Service Center: 888-621-1372
Public Records and Bankruptcies (Diane Cogan): 770-752 1151
Public Records and Bankruptcy Fax: 770-752-1143
Fraud Department Fax Number: 406-802-5672
Data Services (Ward Everett): 770-752-1150
Strategic Anaylsis (Sherry Harper): 770-752-1152
Data Acquisition (Shawn Degray): 770-752-1156
Legal Department (Melody Creswell) 678-795-7947

TransUnion

Switchboard: 312-258-1717
Main Number: 800-888-4213
Ordering System: 800-916-8800
Consumer Relations: 610-546-4600
Consumer Relations Manager (Mary Lane): 610-546-4618
Sales Office (Cathy Rickley): 770-396-7011
Public Records Manager (Rosa Perez): 312-985-3322
Public Records Fax: 312-466-8517
Mailroom: 312-985-4707
Mailroom Manager (Tom Pazur): 312-985-3129
Marketing Department: 800-335-9888
Fraud Victim Assistance Department: 800-680-7289
Fax: 610-546-4758
Consumer Relations Manager Fax (Bonnie Saunder): 610 546-4758
Consumer Protection Department: 714-680-7226
Tour Manager (Melissa Rush): 610-546-4754
Fraud Victim Assistance Manager (Steve Reger): 714-870 5565
Fraud Department Fax: 714-525-0166
Recovery Support Fax: 309-828-8831

Innovis Data Solutions

Switchboard: 614-222-4343
Consumer Relations: 800-540-2505
Mortgage Database: 714-777-2022

ADDRESSES TO THE CREDIT BUREAUS

This section will provide you with the addresses for each of the three major credit bureaus. Some of these addresses are for different locations that each credit bureau has established for the purpose of handling different items on your credit report such as bankruptcies, public records, and delinquent and fraudulent accounts. Please remember each time you are dealing with an account that is fraudulent or you suspect it to be fraud, you want to dispute that item along with your police report and address it to the fraud department of each credit bureau. Send each item by certified mail.

Equifax
1525 Windward Concourse
Mail Drop J69A
Alpharetta, GA 30005

Equifax Credit Information Service
5505 Peachtree Dunwoody Road, Suite 600
P.O. Box 740241
Atlanta, GA 30374-0241

Equifax Information Services
P.O. Box 105518
Atlanta, GA 30348

Equifax Information Services LLC
P.O. Box 740256
Atlanta, GA 30374-0256

Equifax Information Services LLC
P.O. Box 740241
Atlanta, GA 30374

Equifax Utilities & Telecommunications
P.O. Box 105832
Atlanta, GA 30348

Attention: Office of Fraud Assistance
Equifax Information Services LLC
P.O. Box 105069
Atlanta, GA 30348-5069

TransUnion
www.transunion.com
www.transunion.com/investigate

TransUnion Credit Information
555 W. Adam Street
4th Floor
Chicago, IL 60661

TransUnion Consumer Relations
P.O. Box 2000
Chester, PA 19022-2000

TransUnion
Fraud Victim Assistance Department
P.O. Box 6790
Fullerton, CA 92834-6790

TransUnion Consumer Relations
1561 E. Orangethorpe Avenue
Fullerton, CA 92831-5207

TransUnion
P.O. Box 390
Springfield, PA 19064

Experian
475 Anpon Bouvlevard
Building C3
Costa Mesay, CA 92626

Experian
NCAC
P.O. Box 9595
Allen, TX 75013

Experian
Consumer Fraud Assistance
P.O. Box 1017
Allen, TX 75013

Experian
701 Experian Parkway
Allen, TX 75013

Experian
P.O. Box 949
Allen, TX 75013-0949

Experian
Consumer Fraud Assistance
P.O. Box 9532
Allen, TX 75013

Experian Credit Information Service
P.O. Box 2104
Allen, TX 75013

Innovis Data Solutions
250 East Town Street
Columbus, OH 43085

Innovis Data Solutions
950 Threadneedle Streets, Suite 200
Houston, TX 77079

Innovis Data Solutions
5660 New Northside Drive
Northwest Suite 1400
Atlanta, GA 30328

Innovis Data Solutions *(aka CBC Companies)*
5843 Kellog Drive
Yorba Linda, CA 92886

GLOSSARY

Account inquiries—a request for information involving credit history.

Affiliate credit institutions—a branch or group of companies connected as members to a business of origin.

Agents—one who is authorized to act for or in place of another as a business representative.

Authorized user—a person invested, especially with legal authority to have same privileges as primary authority.

Bank—an establishment for the custody, loan, exchange, or issue of money for the extension of credit, and for facilitating the transmission of funds.

Bankruptcy—a person who has done any of the acts that by law entitle his creditors to have his estate administered for their benefit.

Car sweep—used by insurance companies.

Charge-offs—to treat as a loss or expense.

Comprehensive loss underwriting exchange (CLUE)—a claim history information exchange that enables insurance companies to access prior claim information in the underwriting and rating process.

Consumer Credit Protection Act—a law enacted by congress to protect consumers from unfair credit practices that regulates credit reporting agencies, collection agencies, and creditors.

Consumer reporting agencies—compiles and maintains files on consumers nationwide. It regularly engages in the practice of assembling or evaluating and maintaining information about a person's creditworthiness, credit standing, or credit capacity to third parties. Also known as credit bureaus.

Credit repair agency—a company that provides a service to restore credit worthiness and remove bad debt from a consumer's credit report.

Databank—a computer system that specializes in the professional storage, transportation, and management of corporate data.

Database—a large collection of data organized especially for rapid search and retrieval (as by a computer).

Database vendors—companies that sell large collections of data stored for the purpose of rapid search and retrieval.

Employee ID Number—also known as a federal tax identification number: used to identify a business entity.

E-OSCAR—a web-based, automated system that enables data furnishers and credit reporting agencies to create and respond to consumer credit history disputes.

Equal Credit Opportunity Act—prohibits credit discrimination on the basis of race, color, religion, national origin, sex, or martial status.

Fair and Accurate Credit Transaction Act—this act amends the Fair Credit Reporting Act to protect identity theft victims, to place fraud alerts on their credit files, and allow consumers to work with creditors and credit bureaus to prevent the retention of fraudulent information on their credit reports.

Fair Credit Billing Act—designed to protect the consumer against inaccurate and unfair credit billing and credit card practices.

Fair Credit Reporting Act—used to promote accuracy and ensure the privacy of the information used in consumer reports.

Fair Debt Collection Practices Act—enacted to protect consumers from unfair and deceptive debt collection practices.

Federal Trade Commission—independent agency of the U.S. government established in 1915 and charged with keeping American business competition free and fair.

File freeze—a security freeze that allows consumers to stop the sharing of credit with potential creditors.

Identity theft—a crime in which someone wrongfully obtains and uses another person's personal data in some way that involves fraud or deception, typically for economic gain.

Metropolitan Statistical Area—a geographical location used to examine a population or race of people with similar characteristics.

Miscellaneous incident report—a non-crime report submitted for information purposes only.

Pacer system—an electronic public access service that allows users to obtain case and docket in formation from Federal Appellate, District and Bankruptcy courts, and from the U.S. party case index.

Plus/Discount card—membership cards that provide discounts to consumers who shop at certain grocery stores.

Power of attorney—a legal instrument authorizing one to act as the attorney or agent of the grantor.

Secured credit card—to give a pledge of payment to a creditor as collateral to obtain credit.

Tax ID—an identification number used by the Internal Revenue Service in the administration of tax laws. It is issued either by the Social Security administration or the IRS.

Third-party companies—in contract law, a third party is any person or company other than the two principals (the first party and the second party) who is involved in or affected by a contract.

Type A system—consumer's identifying information to be entered into the computer system in an attempt to match existing data if no matching information is found, a new file is created.

Type B system—established mainly on the consumer's Social Security number, Employer Identification Number, or Tax Identification Number. If the consumer's name, address, and zip code do not match the last four digits of the Social Security number that is stored in the database, then a new file is created.

CPSIA information can be obtained
at www.ICGtesting.com
Printed in the USA
LVHW041005280323
742812LV00017B/199